Memories of Finzean

Remarkable stories from her childhood. Chrissie was a member of a large family who lived in Royal Deeside, Aberdeenshire. School was three and a half miles away at Finzean, a journey over cart tracks, through farmyards and over rough moorland. Although the journey was long, it was an interesting and sometimes exciting daily return trip, which one winter very nearly ended in tragedy.

Apart from the dangers they encountered, Finzean was a very special place to be in the nineteen twenties and early thirties. Joseph Farquharson, R.A. was laird of Finzean and prints of his paintings, in particular of his snow and sheep scenes are still selling well today. The laird was a friendly and generous man. The stories of the school, schoolchildren, the laird and the countryside are told using the art of the old style of story telling, which has almost died out. I challenge anyone to read all of these stories without smiling or shedding a tear.

Ruby, (Chrissie's daughter.)

Memories of Finzean

Schooldays 1925 – 1933

Chrissie Gibson

Chrissie Gibson

Braw Promotions (Grampian)

Front cover:

Hares photograph supplied by Aberdeen Journals Ltd

Lang Stracht

Aberdeen

AB15 6DF

Edited by R. Gibson Forbes

First Published 1997 by
Braw Promotions (Grampian)

ISBN 0 9531573 0 X

Printed by
Cordfall Ltd.
0141 332 4640

Contents

CHRISSIE

Introduction

There are many stories of my younger years, such as my schooling, that I would like to write down; if only I could see to do it. Blindness seems to concentrate my mind on memories of my childhood, giving me a clearer picture of a lifestyle long gone. When I die, all of these tales of my early experiences will die with me. It's a shame, as they would make interesting reading.

I have often in recent years, said this to members of my family; but did not think they would take me seriously. I told my daughter Ruby this in a recent telephone conversation. Ruby decided that it was time my stories were recorded and a few days later she turned up with a pen and notepaper, and asked me to dictate stories of my memories of Finzean School from my first day.

The school, much as I first saw it
as we ran up the last half mile

My First Day at School – October, 1925

I remember the first day I went to school, with my three elder brothers. The school was about three and a half miles away, over rough ground and farm tracks. Because of the distance, we were excused school for the first year. I was two months short of my sixth birthday when I started school in October 1925. It was just after the "Tattie Picking Holiday". The idea was to start then instead of January, to get used to the journey before winter set in. When we left for school at about eight o'clock, it was still dark but the sky was getting lighter. I had no idea of what school would be like, or of the journey that lay ahead, so I had been looking forward to starting school. I thought it was a great day.

All my clothes were new. Warm winter clothes – new high boots which laced up to the knees; a deep burgundy winter coat, with fur trimmed collar and cuffs; and matching fur trimmed hat and muff. The muff had a cord which fitted under my coat collar. I also had mitts, to use with my muff when it was really cold.

Both my parents told me that I would really need warm winter clothes and boots during the wintry days. Of course I was too young to understand why they were concerned. I tended to have bronchitis and inflamed glands in my neck in winter. Children even then, were more susceptible to childhood illnesses during their first year at school. Even measles was considered to be a serious illness in those days, and there were no antibiotics. At times we were glad of my father's army first aid/medical training. He always knew what to do for illnesses or accidents.

We set off in high spirits. I was so pleased with my appearance, in particular with the look of my new winter boots, that I didn't realise how heavy the boots were. My legs were tired after the first mile. I wanted to sit down and rest, but Donald, my eldest brother, said "You can't stop, you've only gone a quarter of the way."

Donald almost begged me to get going, telling me that he would have to carry me to school if I didn't get up and walk. "We can't be late for school," he insisted. I wouldn't force my brother to carry me to school, so I just had to go on.

We came to a farm which I imagined was the school, but we only walked through the yard. I also imagined the next farmyard we walked through was the school. I hoped every farm we came to was the school, then we came to rough moorland and I could tell there was about a mile of moor paths before the next farm.

A farm-track led from this farm to the main road. I thought I would never get there.

By now other children were joining us, which encouraged me to go on. When we reached the main road there was still about half a mile to go, but I could see the children ahead of us running to school and knew we would have to run too, to get there on time.

I hung my coat on a peg in the school porch and waited there with the other new children. The teacher rang a handbell in the playground and the other children, starting with the youngest group, trooped past us and took their places in the classroom.

While we waited for the teacher to allot seats to us, I looked around the room. The bench seats had double desks, with one double lid. There were two older children, or three younger children to a bench. Schoolbags were put on the floor.

There seemed to be all ages in the teacher's classroom, with two blackboards. One blackboard was for infants and upwards, to seven or eight years. The second blackboard was for older children. The classroom seemed to be full. There were children at almost every desk. I had never seen so many children in one place before.

There was another room, the headmaster's classroom. My brother Donald was in the top group of the headmaster's class. He was thirteen years old, which meant he would be leaving on his next birthday. Bill and Davie were in the teachers class with me.

That first day, like all other days, started with a prayer and a hymn. Our teacher, Miss Gill, accompanied herself on the piano, but first it had to be uncovered. Two of the older boys, aged about eleven or twelve years, went to what looked like a large crate against the wall. Together they lifted the lid and pushed it back against the wall. Then they lowered the front of the box to the floor. Inside the crate was an old upright piano, with ornate brass candle sticks which folded back against the front of the piano. Miss Gill walked over the box front, and sat at the piano. She accompanied the morning hymn which we all seemed to enjoy singing, and I felt it was a nice way to start the school day.

Miss Gill was a talented pianist, but the piano seemed to me to be very loud, almost deafening. It may have been something to do with the box. The piano was against the wall, and the enclosed ends may have helped to throw the sound out, into the classroom. After the hymn, the same two boys closed the piano's box again. The box was so big that they could hardly reach the lid. It seemed to be made out of plain, unvarnished but dressed wood.

Our teacher was little and elderly, with a raised platform sole on one boot. I thought even then, that she looked very old-fashioned. She always wore black or navy dresses, with long wide sleeves which had neat fitting cuffs. Her dresses had full length skirts and she wore spectacles with little round lenses.

Miss Gill recorded our names on the register, and told us to answer "present" when our names were called. She then read out the whole register.

My brother Donald prepared me for school by teaching me

to write the alphabet, my name, and how to count to a hundred. He told me I had to learn this before going to school, as I would be at a disadvantage starting school a year late.

My first lesson was the alphabet. Miss Gill called out the letters in alphabetical order. We had to raise our hand at each letter we recognised, then write the letter on our slate, which our parents provided. On that first day miss Gill praised me for my knowledge of the alphabet.

Playtime lasted quarter of an hour. Donald asked one of the older girls to take me to the toilet. The school toilets smelled strongly of disinfectant. Although there was a door on the toilet block, there were no doors on the toilet cubicles.

The seats were like wooden boxes, with a round hole cut in the top. The holes were rather large for the smaller children. I looked for the smallest hole, but they were all the same size. Unfortunately, I looked down the hole and was surprised to see a drop of about ten feet. This made me nervous, but I managed to climb up onto the high wooden seat. Some of the younger children were so small, that they had to be lifted up onto the high wooden seat by the older girls. They seemed to be in real danger of falling through, into the sewage below.

There was the usual string of newspaper squares. Although there was no privacy for us, we were not allowed into the toilet block when the older girls were there.

There were few country schools with flush toilets in those days, but our school toilets were always kept clean and smelled of strong disinfectant. However, it wasn't the sort of place that we wanted to spend much time in.

School for the teacher's class finished at three o'clock. I had to wait with Davie and Bill for Donald to finish school, so we could go home together. We were allowed to sit at our desks and look at our school books, until the headmaster's class came out. Going back home, we tried to be back before it was dark so we ran most of the way.

On our way to school there were interesting birds, animals and other sights. However, on my first day, I was too excited to notice any of this on the way to school, and too tired to notice on the way back.

Some of the farmers had gates on their land which had to be opened and closed behind us. Other farmers had high, heavy gates which were left closed. These gates had high wooden or stone stiles, over dry-stane dykes. They all seemed massive to me, especially when my legs were aching on the way back. As I was small for my age, I was unable to climb over the stiles on my own. I was helped up one side of the stile by Bill, and down the other side by Donald. My brothers' were not tall enough to lift me onto, or off, the top of the stiles.

The journey to school had made me so tired that I had fallen asleep at school, but not for long. The eerie screech of slate pencils kept wakening me.

When we got home we didn't have time to sit about. We had to change out of our school clothes. My beautiful, new tartan dress with its velvet collar, had to be kept for school. When we had changed into older clothes, the mud had to be scraped off our boots with a stick. I had no homework on the first day, so I looked after my two younger brothers, Jimmy and Andy, and also my baby sister Margaret. This allowed my mother to prepare dinner, unhindered.

My legs were still aching at bed-time, and I knew they would feel even worse in the morning. I also knew I would have to do it all again, next day and every day, from now on.

The old smiddy showing the high door which a nineteen hand Clydesdale could enter with ease. Alongside is grandson David, height 6' 2".

The Second Day:
Time to Stare

*A*fter the first day at school I knew what to do. In time the aches and pains went from my limbs. From the second day on I started noticing what was going on in the countryside around me.

The farm-workers were ploughing the ground for the following year's planting. The end of the season ploughing helps keep the weeds down, with a bit of assistance from the frost which also helps break up the soil. There were generally two horses to a plough. The ploughmen would shout words of encouragement to the horses, such as "Hud up loon or bonnie lass." "Come awa' Bess or Jock." Sometimes they'd whistle or sing while they worked. A lot of crows followed the plough, feeding on whatever was being turned over.

While we walked through the farmyards, the farming community were getting on with their work. Sometimes corn was being scattered to feed the hens; milk cattle were being turned into the fields after milking, and we could hear pigs grunting as they fed. Bottle reared orphan lambs would run about the farmyards, even after they were fully grown. They would try and eat the hen's corn. Sometimes farmyard ducks or geese would cross our path on their way to the burn. All of the farms in our area reared turkeys, which were a good source of income in December. Farmyards were very busy places in those days.

These were some of the sights and sounds we encountered while hurrying on our way to school. There were also dogs about the farmyards so we had to walk, not run through, or we could chance being bitten. In time we got to know the collies and called out their names as we passed. My favourite was Flossie, who walked beside us through her farmyard and ran beside us until we reached the gate at the end of their land. Somehow I felt as if she was trying to protect us.

I was so tired on my first day at school that I couldn't remember the dinner break, or the afternoon lessons. On the second day I thought I was going home at dinner time.

School dinners were a penny for each child from a family of less than four, or three pence for a family. The only warm place in the school was the soup kitchen, where our dinners were served. I went to the soup kitchen expecting thick wholesome soup, like Mother gave us. The thin, watery soup was hot and that's about all that could be said in its favour. My mother always gave us a thick doorstep of bread to keep us going throughout the day, as there was no sustenance in the soup.

On cold or wet days it was a relief to be warm for twenty or thirty minutes, before going out to the playground shelter. The open sided tin shelters were cold and the classrooms were not much warmer. We shared the shelters with bicycles, so there wasn't much room to play. Few children lived near enough to the school to go home at dinner time, so in heavy rain the shelters were very crowded.

Warm, heavy clothing was a necessity for children in our area, who travelled a long distance to school. Although short trousers were worn by some boys, my brothers and some of the other boys wore breeches. Theirs were navy breeches, which came down to just below the knee and were overlapped by long, thick socks. They also wore short, lacing boots all year long. A waistcoat was worn over a jumper and a heavy jacket was worn over the waistcoat. They wore a white muffler at the neck, but they didn't usually wear a hat. In severe weather conditions their heads were covered by sou'westers. However, on my second day at school it was dry and mild, which gave me a chance to enjoy the journey home.

On the way home we used to stop at the smiddy if any horses were being shod. This was a new experience for me. I watched as the hot horseshoe was held onto the hoof, leaving a mark and burning a shallow bed in the horse's hoof, which caused a smell of burning.

The hoof was trimmed by a very sharp special tool, with a hook. This was used to trim odd bits off the hoof. The hot shoe was then fitted and if a good fit, a piece was trimmed at the front of the hoof to take a point of the shoe. All this time they kept reheating the shoe and if necessary, hammering it into the right shape to make a proper fit. They also had to make holes in the shoe for the nails. The shoe was then put it in a tub of water, until it was cold, then it was nailed onto the hoof.

The nails were hammered in at a slant, coming out through the sides of the hard hoof. The nails were then trimmed and the ends twisted, to prevent ragged ends. Finally the nail ends were gently hammered flat. The farrier talked soothingly to the horse all the time. He had a wonderful way with horses and also with children. He never seemed to mind us watching him while he worked, but he always reminded us to stay well back from the sparks. Then he continued talking to the horse and telling the horse how good the shoe was going to feel. These work-horses were always quiet and well behaved. I felt the horses knew that the smith was caring for their feet when he replaced the shoes. Nearly all the children who passed the smiddy on their way home from school went into the blacksmiths shed for a short while, if there were horses to be shod at the time. We stood just inside the door, well away from the sparks. Then we were running home to try and make up for lost time.

We all had something to do, tasks waiting at home for us. My brothers' had to saw, chop and bring in firewood. The living-room fire was lit every day of the year, as it was used for cooking and baking. It had a small oven at the side, and a swey to hang pots from. Water had to be carried from an open well. It was supplied by a surface spring and the overflow ran into a burn. The buckets had to be dipped into the well by hand. Our well was about four feet deep so we had to be careful to avoid falling in. We never went to the well on our own when we were little.

It was usual in those days, for the older children to look after the younger children, from the age of about four years. We were also warned we'd be punished if we didn't do what our brothers or sisters told us to do. The first task we were usually taught to do was to rock the baby in the cradle, and to do it gently, not to risk rocking it right over. We learned to work together and help one another, from an early age.

In later years these early lessons helped us to accept instructions and orders at work, or in the armed forces. I also felt it helped me to become a better organiser, better at giving instructions, and a better mother.

The First Snow

bout the end of November in my first school winter, 1925, we had the first snow of that winter. We awoke one morning to several inches of soft snow. I really appreciated my warm clothing and boots that day. My father used to apply a thick layer of dubbin on our boots, to keep our feet dry as long as possible. On really wet ground the water still managed to soak through, but the snow wasn't too bad until it turned to slush.

We left home about a quarter to eight, and were told by Mother "Do not scutter about, go straight to school or you'll be late." The snow made the going heavier, and the stiles were slippy. Extra care always had to be taken in winter, to avoid falling on the sharp stones of the dykes. Although our journey took longer we still managed to get to school on time.

Our classroom was a large room, heated only by a small open fire. No one wanted to be at the top of the class in our school, as they were farthest away from the fire.

The weather gradually got worse, particularly in December. Some days the classroom was so dark that the older laddies were told to light paraffin lamps in the early afternoon. We had a good fall of snow in December, and worse was to come. Rain turned the way to school into a mixture of slush, streams of running surface water and mud. Our feet and legs were soaking long before we reached the school. I was surprised when our teacher told us to take off our boots and socks or stockings, saying "I don't want you all to get pneumonia."

Miss Gill took a box from the cupboard which was overflowing with grey socks and red slippers. Our socks or stockings were hung up to dry. The boots were arranged round the fire, and we were told to keep turning them now and again, to save them from being burned. Only the children who had to walk a long way to school, were lent socks and slippers.

Miss Gill found time to do this plus our normal lessons. She taught us simple cooking and needlework, while teaching a variety of ages. She still managed to find time to arrange a Christmas concert. We were taught to sing carols, recite, make toffee and decorate the hall.

Few families had a full set of text books. Even asking for a jotter to copy notes from someone else's text book could prompt the reaction from parents of "Do you think I'm made of money." Despite this drawback Miss Gill kept each age group busy throughout each day. Instructions for each class were written on the blackboards, so we knew what we should be doing until she got round to our group.

When the weather seemed to be getting worse, we had a

half day and were told to go straight home. There was no waiting about for soup, or hanging about with friends. Our lives might depend on getting home as quickly as possible. We were also told by our headmaster not to come to school next day if the weather was bad.

When we changed into the school's dry socks, we were told to wear them home with our own boots, and return them another day. The socks picked up black dye from the boots. Mother soaked the dye out of the socks, washed, dried and pressed each pair which we returned a few days later.

One morning we awoke to find the snow was too deep to chance going to school by the usual route. My oldest brother Tommy hitched our horse to an old horse-sleigh, which Father kept for emergencies. It was possible to be cut off from the nearest shop for a few days when the road was too dangerous to risk driving a cart or carriage on. Tommy hung a bell on the horse to warn other travellers we were coming, as it takes longer to stop a sleigh. Our journey to school by the main road, a distance of about five miles, was great fun.

When we got near the school the other children waved and laughed as we passed. Some of them ran along behind us, trying to keep up. Tommy was only about sixteen years old at the time, and he had a great sense of fun. We really enjoyed the trip to school that morning and it only took half the usual time

When the school came out we still had to walk home by the usual route, but the farmers had made paths in the snow when they went to feed their animals. The moorland path was too deep, but we could see where the snow drifts were as the wind usually blew the snow towards the mountainside. It left what was almost a natural pathway where the snow wasn't too deep.

Going to school by horse-sleigh is one of my favourite memories, but it was a rare event.

Old Finzean school before 1964 while still in use as a school.

Approaching Christmas

*M*y first Christmas at Finzean School was a mysterious and exciting time, as like many families in our area we did not celebrate Christmas. Miss Gill taught us Christmas hymns. The first I learned was "Away In A Manger", which to this day is my favourite Christmas hymn.

Miss Gill accompanied herself on the piano, while she sang the hymn to us. First she pointed to the words, which were written on the blackboard, while we sang. Then we sang along with Miss Gill and the piano. She advised the older children to practice from their hymn books, at home. The singing lessons were really for the older children, who could already read and write, but I picked up the words quickly and joined in. Miss Gill didn't seem to mind as I had finished the work set for us. She always encouraged musical interest in her pupils.

Even then, I loved the old Christmas hymns and carols. On

the way home from school I sang them with my brothers and other children, who walked part of the way home with us. We all enjoyed singing, and it seemed to bring that special Christmas atmosphere to our homeward journey. The journey seemed shorter and our steps were lighter.

Miss Gill had a variety of quaint sayings and expressions which helped us remember our lessons. About this time some of the children seemed to have difficulty remembering the tunes, and complained that they couldn't do it. "Nonsense", was Miss Gill's reply. "Put a stout heart to a steep brae and you'll soon waddle up it." When the children she'd spoken to got it right she praised their efforts, telling them how they had been "Putting a stout heart to the task". She instilled a feeling of pride in her pupils' singing, which made us all keen to take part in the "Christmas Concert".

It was a very busy time of the year for us, as most of the classes were involved either in practising for the school concert, making colourful paper decorations for the school and the village hall, or being involved in fund raising. Sometimes we got out early, as the older girls were making Swiss milk toffee to sell. There was a raffle, which my father always contributed a prize to. One year he contributed the star prize of an English bone china tea set. The older children went round the area selling raffle tickets and money was also raised by charging an entrance fee for "The Nativity Play And Concert".

The Nativity play, and a number of musical numbers, were practised until perfect. Some of the costumes were made out of coloured paper. Miss Gill was an excellent needlework and craft-work teacher. It amazed me that the paper costumes looked so good. She seemed to be able to do a lot with a little. I was not allowed to take part in the school concert during my first year at school, as it was held in the evening, and I was too young to be out that late. The school concert was shown first in the headmaster's classroom, in front of the school. I enjoyed the concert and was keen to take part, but I had to wait until I was eight years old. The atmosphere of excitement grew as we got nearer the end of term, and "The Laird's Christmas Party".

"The Laird's Christmas Party" was held for his workers, his tenants, their families, and the children of "Finzean School". "Finzean School" had at one time been the "Finzean Estate School" and the Laird continued to take an interest in the school. We had a half day on the last day of term. We all walked in a line to "Finzean House" which was about half a mile away. I knew that this was going to be a very special occasion, as the older children had been looking forward to this day for weeks. Soon I would find out why everyone thought the party was the most special event of their year.

The Laird's Christmas Party

The Laird's Christmas parties were held in the ballroom, above the stables at Finzean House. As we climbed the stairs to the hall, we were all very excited. I knew this was going to be a special occasion and was told that the laird's wife would greet us, just inside the doorway, at the top of the stairs.

The first impression I had of Lady Violet Farquharson was of her perfume which rivalled the finest scents of any flower garden. She welcomed us in a warm, cheerful way and I was struck by how attractive her hair was. She always wore her hair up, but not in an ordinary bun. I can't describe her hair, but if I tried, I know the description would not do her hair justice.

Before I had the chance to take in more of this fine lady's appearance, she handed me a paper bag full of cakes. I followed the others into the hall and peeped into the bag. There were five or six delicious looking cakes. On top was an iced, cream bun and a doughnut, with an iced fruit slice below. I ate some of the cakes with a large mug of tea, which I really enjoyed. As I drank my tea, I looked round the brightly decorated hall. Paper decorations hung from the ceiling, and paper garlands, with holly, decorated the walls. There were lots of bright red holly berries. However, we had not yet seen the tree.

After tea the stage curtains were opened and I was introduced for the first time to a Christmas tree. It was a magnificent Christmas tree by any standards. To me it was like being transported to a wonderful fairyland. I don't remember particular decorations, just that it was brightly lit and seemed to shimmer of gold and silver. The tree was surrounded by many, beautifully wrapped gifts. The youngest children were first to receive their gifts. The laird called my name first. He seemed such a nice man that I went forward for my gift, without being nervous.

"What would you like for Christmas, Christina?"

I didn't want to choose a gift in case it was too much, so I told the laird I didn't know.

"Would you like a doll?" I nodded.

"I have a very special doll for you, Christina. It's the most beautiful of all the dolls." He handed me a box wrapped in Christmas paper. My first real Christmas gift, so beautifully wrapped and with my name card attached.

There was a gift of outstanding quality for each child. All the gifts seemed to be chosen with care, as they were all suitable and appreciated by each child. My brother Davie, when he got home, found he had a toy horse and cart which he enjoyed playing with and sharing with our younger brothers. The oldest boys who would soon be leaving school, were given a choice of a gift, or money. Donald was offered either a mouth-organ or half a crown. (12 ½ new pence, or two shillings and sixpence.) Donald choose the money, as he already had a mouth-organ.

The laird, Joseph Farquharson, was already an old man of seventy nine years, in 1925. He didn't seem to have any children of his own, but over the years he made a great deal of children happy. At that first party, I wondered if he realized just how much the party and gifts meant to us, or just how happy he made all of us. Ordinary people had so little to enjoy or treasure in their lives that the laird's parties, his gifts and general kindness to everyone he met, were appreciated far more than today's affluent and cossetted society could imagine. Mere words can't describe how the local people of Finzean felt about Lord and Lady Farquharson.

After the gifts were presented, the laird was thanked by a representative of his workers. Then it was time to go home. Two hours had flown past so quickly that I couldn't believe it was over. We were each given an apple and an orange to put in our schoolbags, when it was time to leave.

My journey home was exciting, as I tried to imagine my doll. We discussed everything we would remember to tell the others about, when we got home. The walk of over four miles seemed to be over in no time. At home we shared the fruit and the remaining cakes with our brothers and sisters, while I tried to describe the hall and the fabulous Christmas tree.

The best moment was still to come and was well worth waiting for. Now it was time to open my Christmas present. It was time to see the doll that the laird had promised me "was the most beautiful of all the dolls".

My Precious Doll

My precious gift was carefully carried home. Unbreakable plastics were a future invention and dolls of that time were all fragile, unlikely to stand being dropped once.

I knew by the size of the box, and the weight of my parcel, that this was going to be a large, expensive doll. When I unwrapped the colourful wrapping paper – slowly, savouring every second – I lifted the lid and was hardly able to believe just how beautiful my doll was. She had real hair, dark brown and curly, and an exquisite face. Her beautifully made clothes and underwear were made to be removed and replaced many times, and were washable. Even her shoes fitted. Carefully I lifted her out of the box and cradled her in my arms, then I wondered if there was something wrong with her eyes; they appeared to be closed. I lifted her into an upright position and had a wonderful surprise when she opened her eyes to return my gaze.

Her eyes were realistic, sleeping eyes, which opened and

closed when she was tipped over. This must have been a recent innovation as I didn't know anyone else that had a doll like this before the party. When I tipped her back to watch her eyes, I had another surprise when she said "Ma Ma".

My parents were very impressed by the doll. Father said that it was "well worth keeping". Within a few days, father had made a special wooden box for my doll. The box was made like a piece of furniture, of stained and polished wood. It had a glass door and he fitted it to our living-room wall, where both the doll and its display box were much admired by visitors. In fact, although my mother was not short of ornaments, or pictures, the doll took pride of place in our house.

Whenever an adult was there, I was allowed to play with the doll. I just had to ask for one of my parents or older brothers or sisters to take it out for me. My younger brothers and sisters were not allowed to play with my doll, as my father knew they wouldn't treat it with the same care as I always did. I spent many happy hours playing with my special doll, for about three years. Unfortunately, my younger brother Jimmy, who was about four years old at the time, became fascinated by the "Ma Ma" sound that the doll made. He wanted to find out what made the noise.

One day when no one was about, Jimmy dragged a chair over to the doll's box. He was now able to reach the doll, as father had not thought it necessary to fit a lock on the door. Jimmy removed the doll and smashed it to pieces. I couldn't believe that my doll had gone forever. I sobbed off and on for hours. Although Father was very angry with Jimmy, I knew that he would only be told off for the damage he'd caused.

Jimmy was considered to be a weak child, and was never smacked for anything he did. This time I decided that I would punish him by not speaking to him. I was so hurt over the destruction of my treasured doll that I didn't speak to him for ages afterwards. Well it felt like ages to both of us, it was probably only for a few days.

As I spent more time than my brothers caring for the younger ones, and keeping them amused, they became more attached to me. Jimmy followed me about begging me to speak to him again. Of course he didn't realize when he broke the doll, just how upset I would be. The doll was irreplaceable. It was the most wonderful doll in the whole world. Never again would I love any object, any non-living thing, the way I loved that doll.

The Festive Season

fter the excitement of "The Christmas Party", our holiday was probably the best of "The Festive Season Holidays" that I had during my school days. The frosty weather continued throughout the school break, giving me the opportunity to learn ice skating.

My father bought two pairs of old ice skates at a roup (country auction). They were the kind of skates which were strapped on to boots or shoes. They were to fit adults, but Bill, Donald and Tommy managed to skate with them. Davie found them a bit clumsy and heavy, but there was no way they could adjust them to fit me. Bill solved the problem by making me a wooden pair. They were great to skate in, much lighter than the real ice skates but just as good. A second pair was made for Davie, so four of us could skate at once.

Our ice rink was a hollow in the hills where surface water tended to collect, but it wasn't deep enough to be dangerous. Our skating was completely natural, as we had never seen anyone else skate, although we had heard of it and seen pictures of people skating in books. The need to skate took over our lives for a short while. We knew the ice was only temporary, so we spent every spare minute skating.

For most of that holiday my parents hardly saw us. We would rush through our daily tasks, and slip out before Mother thought of anything else she wanted us to do. Our time was spent in our personal skating rink where we had lots of fun. We only went home at meal times and, when darkness fell, we skated by moonlight. We would hear father whistling for us at bed time, or I think we would have skated all night long. I never had any difficulty sleeping in those days.

Christmas day was just another day to us as "New Years Day" is traditional gifts day in the "North of Scotland". We had a special dinner on "Hogmanay", the last day of the year. We hung up our stockings beside the fire and were just as excited as any child is on "Christmas Eve". Our stockings on "New Years Day" contained modest gifts, in keeping with the time we lived in. We had an apple, an orange, sweets, pencils, jotters, and a small toy. Most people had large families and small incomes so few children fared better than we did. We enjoyed the festive atmosphere, and the way people seemed to be so much nicer to one another at this time.

There were no loud parties on "Hogmanay", or the early hours of "New Years" morning. Visitors tended to call round during the day. My father's friend and his two sons were good fiddlers. They arrived in the afternoon. Father had whisky for guests, but there was no serious drinking, this was a musical occasion. Father brought out his bagpipes and played a few tunes, the fiddlers played and my mother, who had a beautiful singing voice, sang a variety of old traditional ballads. Then there were popular songs, which the whole family joined in singing.

Mother always spent more time baking for the festive season. There were extra scones, pancakes and cakes, and a special meal again on the 1st of January. My favourite was the fruit duff. It was a light, fruit, steamed pudding; which also contained a few silver coins wrapped in grease-proof paper parcels. This added more fun and laughter to a delicious meal.

Soon it was time to go back to school. The weather seemed to be changing and deep snow would soon cover our ice rink. By the end of the holiday I didn't really mind going back as I wanted to learn to read and write, and also to see my friends at school. I was also curious to see what happened during the rest of the school year, at school and on the way there.

The Storm

$\mathcal{M}$issing the first year at school due to living over three miles from the school meant that it was essential to be there every single day; apart from severe illnesses or dangerous weather conditions. Even when it was snowing we tried to get in half a day's tuition. This determination to get to school almost cost us our lives.

The winter of 1925/26, was a particularly bad one. Early in 1926, probably just a week or two into the Spring term, we left for school one morning while it was snowing. It was a light fall of snow, which had been falling steadily for an hour or two. We left for school, as usual, before daylight; which didn't give Father much time to asses the weather situation. After a while we realized the snow fall was getting heavier. Bill wanted to turn back, but Donald was older and said. "Snow or rain before seven, off by eleven." So we carried on.

The farmers were taking their beasts in from the fields, and leaving the gates open. This avoided snow drifting against the gates and blocking the entrances to the fields. Bill felt that this was a sure sign that it wasn't safe to go on. Donald was in charge and he decided we would go on.

The snow was getting deeper and the wind stronger as it howled eerily over the moor. I found the sound of the wind threatening as it was louder and stronger than it had ever been before. We hurried on until we finally arrived at the school. Few children had gone to school and the headmaster closed the school, after an hour or two. We were told to hurry home as it seemed as if a storm was due. Outside the weather was getting worse.

The snow was falling thick and fast and the wind was even stronger as we ran up the road. By the time we reached the moor, it was a whiteout. The usual path was impossible to find, and the snow drifts were too deep there anyway. As we could only see for a foot or two around us, we crossed the moor by feeling our way along the dyke, which ran the length of the moor. The wind on the moor swirled the snow round and round, threatening to choke us. All the time the wind screamed like the voices of an attacking army, screaming for the blood of the enemy. I desperately wanted to find shelter of some kind to hide in, but Donald kept insisting that we had to go on. He knew the cold would kill us if we stopped.

Before we reached the gate we normally used when leaving the moor, we found our way was blocked by a massive snowdrift, as the gate had not been left open. If we tried to go round it we might not find our way off the moor, and become trapped in deep snow. Donald lifted me onto the top of the dyke, then he lifted Davie and Bill onto the dyke. Davie and Bill helped Donald to climb up beside us. The snow on the other side was level with the top of the dyke. Our only hope was to walk along the top of the dyke, until we could find a way down.

A thick layer of snow covered the top of the dyke, so we couldn't even choose steadier stones to step on. I walked between Donald and Bill. They tried to protect me from the worst of the wind, as it tried to pluck us off the wall; which would result in us being smothered in deep snow. As I was small and thin for my age, Donald tried to protect me by offering to carry me along the top of the dyke on his back. I refused, as I didn't want to pull him off the dyke with me. All this time the wind seemed to be getting louder, stronger and colder.

We came to a wider section of dyke, where stones cleared from the land were dumped, at a junction of dykes. Donald had planned to get off here, thinking that there would be a lower level of snow at some point here. Unfortunately there was no way down, we were surrounded by a massive snowdrift. At this point Donald almost gave up. He looked round this heap of stones and said "Oh my God, we'll never mack it hame." My tears at these words brought reassurance from Donald and Bill that we would get home somehow.

Now I was so cold and tired that I just wanted to lie down and sleep. The next section of dyke was topped by barbed wire, but we couldn't go back as the snow on the moor was now much deeper. The barbed wire seemed to make the task impossible. Then, as I wished my father was there to take us home, I thought I heard him whistle. I thought I heard the whistle signal he always used when calling us when we were out of sight.

Father's whistle usually carried a long distance. Now with the wind for competition, I was sure I had imagined it. There it was again, or was it. I wanted my father so much, that it must be my imagination. Then Bill heard it too. We knew Father must be waiting for us, beside the dyke, where the snow wasn't so deep.

We set off along the dyke, trying to avoid the barbed wire. After a while we could hear father calling our names. When we reached him he was on the other side of the barbed wire. Father had cleared a path through a deep snowdrift, to get to this part of the dyke. He told Donald to step on the wire to hold it down while he lifted me down. Then it was Davie and Bill's turn to be lifted off the dyke. Donald wanted to jump down but Father was afraid his boot would catch on the wire. Donald was told to put his hands on Father's shoulders, while Father lifted him clear of the wire. I felt safe at last, I knew we would get home, but Father was crying with relief. He cuddled all of us, hardly able to believe we were alive.

Donald went ahead, clearing a path to a small wood nearby, which my father carried me to. He cleared the thick layer of snow from our clothes in the shelter of the wood. From there the road was slightly easier, as a road to the next farm had dykes either side, which prevented drifts forming. Father was wearing a long heavy coat. He covered my head and shoulders with the front flap on one side, and Davie, who was eight at the time, was sheltered by the flap on the other side. Donald and Bill tried to shelter behind us, but the swirling wind was nearly suffocating whatever we did to avoid it.

The remainder of our journey was still difficult, but once we were through the next farmyard the snow wasn't quite so deep. The farmers had cleared some of the snow earlier, to move their beasts and the roads were more sheltered there. Finally we made it home to our warm fireside and a hot meal. The snow continued throughout the rest of that day and night, and well into the next day. It was said by some people to be the worst storm in living memory. I can only describe the way it happened. I can't describe the relief I felt on seeing my father, or on reaching our home.

I wonder now, just how long my father stood waiting for us? If he had assumed that we must have sought shelter at one of the farms, or assumed that we must have taken the longer, but less hazardous main road then we would have died before reaching home. The visibility was so poor that we could have easily lost our way. Thankfully, Donald took the right decisions on our way home, but he was very sorry that he didn't turn back on our way to school.

My parents discussed our brush with death and decided never again to take the chance of that happening. Our well being was more important than our education. If it was snowing early in the morning, then we stayed at home.

Donald Leaves School

*M*ost of the severe weather was past when Donald reached his fourteenth birthday, in February. That was the last day of school for Donald, and a very sad day for us. Donald tried to help us by giving us the following advice. "Stick together, help one another, always do what the eldest one tells you to do. Look after your younger brothers and sisters, when they start school."

We were a large family and had no other relatives living nearby. Neither of our parents came from the Finzean area, so we knew we had to depend on one another and help one another. Only people who are brought up within large families know how close we were to one another.

Donald took very good care of us when he was at school, but Bill made us more independent; made us think for ourselves. If we tended to hang about on the way to school, he would just say, "O.K. make yourselves late." He would then break into a run and of course we ran after him. In this way he encouraged us to take more responsibility for our own actions.

Donald was clever enough to have gone on to Banchory Academy, to complete his education. However, my father couldn't afford the extra expense of not only the textbooks, but the cost of accommodation during the stormy weather, for several weeks in winter. Father could have paid for some of us to go to the Banchory school, but he believed in treating us all equally. Even his daughters were treated more or less as equals to his sons. Although for our own safety, we had less freedom.

My brothers were all taught to cook to the same standard as their sisters. We daughters were taught to handle a horse and gig, or cart, and encouraged to learn to drive when we were old enough. Father was a very unusual man for his day.

The Yo-Yos

Shortly after Donald left school, children started taking home-made yo-yos to school. They were made out of either two large coat buttons sewn together, or a sliced, wooden cotton reel; which was joined by a wooden dowel. We tried home made yo-yos, but they did not work very well, then our older brothers' gave us better yo-yos, which worked beautifully.

Tommy and Donald were in Aberdeen for the day when they saw brightly coloured yo-yos in Woolworths store. At that time Woolworths still proudly carried the sign of 0/6d. (nothing over six pence) over the door of their shop. My brothers were surprised to find how cheap their yo-yos were. They bought half a dozen (6) for younger brothers and me. I was the only younger sister, apart from the baby.

We were very proud of our yo-yos. Especially as our older brothers had bought them for us. It was pleasing to be the first children in the school to have manufactured yo-yos. Soon many children at our school had Woolies yo-yos, which provided more fun than many expensive toys.

A year or so later there was a craze for hula hoops. Most of these were rings off of imported apple barrels. The hula hoops were more expensive than Woolie's yo-yos, so we just had to make do with the home made type of hoop. It was fun while the craze lasted, but soon our interests had moved to something else. Skipping ropes were popular all the time. The bigger lassies would sometimes include us in their skipping games, telling us to jump alongside of them. The younger boys shared our playground and sometimes joined the girls skipping groups. One year during hot weather, an insane craze started which fortunately only lasted for a short time.

As we wore our winter clothes for school all year round, we suffered from the heat in sunny weather. We even wore boots all year round. It was during a hot spell when one of the older lassies introduced me to the new craze. She approached me in the playground holding a small, bulging, brown paper bag. "Hold out your hand Chrissie, I've got something for you." I was very suspicious as she had no reason to give me anything so at first I refused. In the end my curiosity overcame common sense, and I held my hand out. Slowly and carefully, she placed the bag on the palm of my hand, then suddenly smashed her hand down on mine; showering us both with cold water. I didn't join in the hysterical laughter that followed, but I did notice other children playing tricks with these water bombs.

Next day everyone seemed to have brought paper bags to school. We searched our homes for larger, stronger paper bags, to make bigger splashes. The school's only tap was very busy at break time. There was a long queue of younger children, with bigger children jumping the queue. By the time break was over, I think every child in the school must have been thoroughly soaked. Miss Gill looked shocked at the sight of her soaking class. "What happened? How did you all get wet?" Of course nobody said anything about water bombs. "You're not sitting on my classroom seats soaking wet. Don't any of you dare come into my classroom in that state again."

The water bomb craze ended there and then in school. Although it went on for a short while out of school until our households ran out of paper bags. Our clothes dried quickly in the hot weather. My mother's only comment when we got home was that for once all our hands seemed to be clean when we got home from school. We assumed at the time that Mother didn't know, but I'm sure she must have heard about it eventually.

Miss Gill seemed surprised at our appearance but I doubt if hysterical screaming from over a hundred pupils would have gone unnoticed by Miss Gill, or the headmaster.

Crazes in our school came and went, but I doubt if any of the other crazes were as extreme as our water bomb battles, with the larger bags of water being wielded like pillows in a pillow fight.

An adder, Britain's only poisonous snake.

A Lambskin Coat and a Snakeskin

Sometimes farm animals could prove as interesting as wildlife. One Spring morning during my first school year, I noticed new-born lambs in a field. My attention was drawn to a lamb bleating loudly. I was surprised to see the lamb being pushed away roughly by a sheep. I couldn't understand this, it seemed so cruel. Bill explained to me that the lamb didn't belong to that sheep. "Watch what the sheep does next, and you'll see." The sheep pushed the lamb away, and went to another lamb, which was her own. The bleating lamb was found by its own mother. My brother explained that the sheep knows its own lamb by its scent. Normally a ewe won't accept any other lamb as her own, but shepherds have found a way to use the scent of a still born lamb, to persuade a ewe to foster an orphan lamb.

Once, when I was on my way to school, I saw a shepherd

skinning a still-born lamb. The skin was pulled onto an orphan lamb, like a tight fitting coat; so the still-born lamb's mother, would accept the orphan lamb as her own. After a couple of days, the mother will come to accept the scent of the orphan lamb, which she smells along with the scent of the extra skin. When the skin is removed, she accepts the orphan as her own.

A common sight on our way to and from school were hawks. They would hover, usually high in the sky, and swoop down suddenly making a whoof sound with their wings. Then they would make off with a mouse, a small bird, a young rabbit, or even one of the farmer's chickens. They would be gone almost as quickly as they'd arrived. Golden eagles went for bigger pray – a lamb, a new born deer, a full grown rabbit or hare, a hen, or one of the bigger wild birds. Some people said it might be possible for an eagle to take a small child. Anything that moved, that could be carried away, was fair game to an eagle. Owls were keen mouse hunters. They would also take other birds' chicks. I disliked the eerie hoot or loud shriek of an owl. I also didn't like the way an owl looked at me, almost as if it was thinking of me as possible prey. Even poisonous adders didn't make me feel as uncomfortable as an owl, as it watched my every movement and made me feel as if it could still see me after I was out of sight.

Father taught us to respect snakes, and if possible, to give them a wide berth. The only kind of snakes we saw in Royal Deeside, were poisonous adders. Quite often we'd find discarded snake skins in the heather. Sometimes, there was even a snake basking in the sun, while its skin dried. I have even seen a snake in the process of discarding its skin. It seems to have quite a struggle, forcing the already too tight skin off. Once it starts shedding its skin, it has to carry on until the whole skin is shed. Then it seems to be exhausted, but we still kept well clear of it, as it was still poisonous.

We all managed to avoid being bitten, even when we came across tiny, newly hatched snakes. We used to retrace our steps, and go a long way round as adders are born with a sac full of ready-to-use venom. When we found a recently discarded snake skin, we would pick it up with a stick, have a closer look, then throw it away. The adders never seemed to hang about long after discarding their skin. We were never bored when we travelled to and from school, or wandered about nearby forests or moorland. We didn't stay indoors for long if the weather was reasonable.

At the weekend and in the evenings we kept ourselves amused, and out of our parents way, with whatever was at hand. Sometimes, we would collect a big spider, which we would keep in a jar. Then a variety of live insects would be added to the jar. The spider would spin a silk shroud for its victims, so its food supply would be kept fresh. In this way we produced our own nature programme, long before we saw television for the first time.

The most interesting experiences always seemed to happen on our way to and from school, or during our school dinner break. I used to feel sorry for my cousins, who were not lucky enough to live in the country.

Schoolchildren, c. 1920

Bigfoot
and other Bullies

O ne of the most hurtful experiences I had as a child was the first time I was picked on by one of the big laddies at our school. Unfortunately we had to go through the boys' playground, to girls' playground. It was advisable to stay close to the wall and try and steer clear of laddies fighting. There always seemed to be at least one fight going on in their playground, and usually it involved bigger laddies.

Shortly after I started school I was walking close to the wall, while watching a fierce fight. The fight was fairly close and I was trying to avoid being caught up in it, so I didn't pay much attention to the biggest boy in the school. Although he was only thirteen, this lad was over six foot tall. I didn't imagine that he would pick on a tiny five year old.

While I was walking around him, still watching and worrying about the fight veering in my direction, this giant of a teenager tripped me up. I fell with some force as I was hurrying to get away from the fight. Bigfoot's laughter made the pain in my grazed chin, hands and knees seem much worse. My howls, due to pain and fear of what he would do next brought my brothers to my aid.

Donald and Bill looked suspiciously at my attacker, who continued to lean nonchalantly against the wall. Donald demanded to know what had happened.

"I'm sorry, but she wisna' watching whaur she was gan, and tripped ower my foot."

I looked at this giant towering over my brother Donald, who was tiny then and only grew eventually to about five foot six. I decided to take the blame for being careless, rather than start a very uneven fight. I stayed well clear of "Bigfoot" after that incident, and also Bigfoot's relatives. He came from a family of big handsome men who were all talented musicians with outgoing personalities – not outsiders, or unpopular characters who are pressured into being bullies – they just seemed to enjoy it. After Bigfoot and his brothers and cousins left our school, it became almost a pleasant place to be.

Years later I saw Bigfoot in Banchory, when I was an adult. I didn't have to fear him any more, but I was surprised to be hailed with a cheerful "Hello Chrissie", as if we were old pals. He went on to enquire how my brothers were, and how I was getting along. Suddenly, to my own surprise, I let loose a torrent of feelings, held back for years to avoid trouble. I told him exactly what I thought of him, then with a parting shot of "If you ever see me again don't bother trying to speak to me", I turned abruptly, not waiting for an answer, and walked away, still fuming after all those years.

Other Bullies

There were bullies among the girls too. I would hurry through the boys' playground, hoping to reach the girls toilets before the big lassies got there. They sometimes threatened to push us through the holes, which served as seats, into the sewage below. If I couldn't get there for a quick visit before the older ones, I just had to keep it in until the end of the break. When our teacher rang the bell, I would then rush in for a quick visit, in the hope that I wouldn't get the strap for hanging about.

Sometimes two or three big lassies would surround me, and all punch me. I quickly learned which of the bigger lassies to hang about near, and which to avoid. I also learned very quickly, to lash out at them if they looked like picking on me. I found that if even a small child punches and kicks hard enough to hurt, they are more likely to be left alone.

At other times, there would be a big organised fight which the little ones were expected to join. I chose the side which fought against the cruel, foul-mouthed bullies. I disliked these lassies and wouldn't fight along with them. Swearing was a strapping offence and I didn't want to be associated with their group, by the headmaster. During these big fights I stayed back and tried to avoid trouble. When orphans, known as boarded out children, came to our school they became very unpopular. Some children resented the strangers, who seemed to get preferential treatment. Some of the boarded out children seemed to expect trouble and overacted to any problems they encountered. I found it was better avoiding these children as even trying to be friendly, could result in the strap from our teacher.

About the third or fourth year we had a new headmaster who knew how to handle the bullies. He rarely used the strap, but he made it clear to all pupils that he would not tolerate bullies in his school. Bullies would be expelled. Our new headmaster was well liked by all the children. He was strict but fair and he was an excellent teacher. His lessons were always interesting and he seemed to genuinely care for his pupils.

Larking About

*I*n winter my parents put out food for the robins and crows, which encouraged us to be thoughtful and caring towards creatures in need and ultimately towards one another. Our long journey to and from school gave us the opportunity to appreciate the changing seasons and the effect it has on wildlife.

Towards the end of winter the wildlife became more active. Although we didn't have time to stop and stare on the way to school, we had time to stop for a short while on the way back. If we were very interested then a minute or two was likely to become ten or twelve minutes, which we then tried to make up by running, as we wanted to get home before it was dark.

My favourite time of the year was the first two weeks in March, when the normally timid brown hares become reckless, bold and aggressive. It is easy to understand why they have earned the title of "Mad March Hares". One or more groups of brown hares gather in a field. They give the impression that they are sizing one another up, then one hare selects an opponent and bounds over to confront the rival. Facing one another they rear up on their hind legs, their front legs flailing at one another, like two boxers, until one retreats at high speed.

Bill advised me to stay out of the way of fleeing hares, as they seem to run in blind panic. "You dinna want to be knocked ower by seven or eight pounds o' fleeing hare."

They seemed to have a preference for a field we passed close to on our way to school. The first time I saw hares boxing, they were pointed out to me by Davie. "They're just like laddies fighting at school. They're aggravating one another, wae their pals standing round egging them on. See how the pals bob up and down wae excitement, you wad think they were betting on who's pal would win."

The hares really made the fur fly. Little bits of fluff filled the air round them, like brown and white speckled snow flakes. As we were going to school the "Mad March Hares" could have made me late, but Davie urged me on, "Hurry Chrissie or we'll be late for school, we'll get the strap."

Later in the year, frogs were particularly fascinating to us. They could be found in a quarry pool, not far from our route. The frogs came in a variety of shades of green and brown, and a variety of sizes. With other children who walked part of the way home with us, we watched the frogs mating. When a female had too much attention from the males, she could be overcome by exhaustion. Sinking to the bottom under the weight of a male, she could drown.

Sometimes we would have a competition to see which frog could jump the farthest. A light touch to their rear with a stick would send them leaping in all directions. I always looked for a frog with long legs and a narrow body, as they seemed to jump farther.

There seemed to be far more birds about then, and some species are no longer found in the North East of Scotland. Birds busy nest building reminded us that Summer was on its way. Lapwings, swallows and swifts performed aerobatics at times, building their nests to perfection. Crows carried long twigs to build larger, roughly constructed nests, adding a soft lining later.

Each morning in Spring, we seemed to disturb small birds in a field as we passed by. These tiny birds flew straight up in the sky, chirping loudly and flapping their wings furiously. This only happened in the mornings, so we never had time to see how high they flew, or where they went. Each Spring I longed to find out what they were going to do, but there was never enough time. Finally I felt I just had to see where they were going, and how high they flew. "I dinna care if I'm late", I replied to Davie's warning. "It will be worth having the strap, to see what these little birds do." I lay on my back, in a corner of the field, and stared up at these tiny birds. I thought that if I stayed still for long enough, that the birds would think I had gone. I didn't understand that I would need a camouflaged hide to fool these birds. A burgundy coat and a tartan skirt are a great disadvantage to a bird watcher. After what seemed to me like an age, I just had to carry on to school disappointed and with only the strap to look forward to.

Miss Gill was surprised that my younger brother Andy was on time, but I was late. When I arrived several minutes after the lesson had started, she sounded quite cross.

"Christina, what were you doing that made you late for school?"

I went on to explain with enthusiasm and animation, how I just had to see where these tiny birds went and how high they flew. I described how their shrill song could still be heard clearly when the bird was out of sight, still hovering high above my head. "It didn't come down, or fly away, while I was there."

"What did you learn from this that was worth missing lessons for, Christina?"

I thought about how I could put my feelings into words, then I knew. "I learned what the saying 'Happy as a lark' means, Miss!"

Miss Gill had to laugh at this, and admitted that she had done the same herself. She said that she couldn't find out where they went either. To everyone's surprise she didn't give me the strap on that occasion. Sternly she told me "Don't let this happen again!"

No matter how interesting I thought wildlife was, I never let wildlife make me late for school again.

Easter

I enjoyed hearing the religious stories of Easter, which Miss Gill told. Easter was more of a religious festival in those days and I had never heard of a chocolate egg. An Easter Egg was a hen's egg which was sometimes dyed or painted. We didn't celebrate Easter by going on a picnic because some of our relatives usually visited us on Easter Sunday.

The days were getting longer and brighter when our half day at the start of the holiday came round. I had been looking forward to the Easter holidays, but as it turned out I wasn't in a fit state to enjoy them. I didn't feel well on the last day and I felt very tired on the way home. Soon I was fevered, and then I started vomiting. A rash of blisters on my back worried my parents, so I was taken to visit the doctor at Aboyne.

The journey, in a gig, was very uncomfortable. Every movement added to the pain, so it was a great relief when the return journey was over. I don't actually remember much about the visit, as I was too ill at the time. The doctor diagnosed shingles, which was looked on as an old people's illness. The only way to treat the illness was to keep warm, rest, and apply zinc and castor oil cream to the rash. The doctor said that the further round my chest the rash spread, the longer the illness would last. At that time shingles was thought to be caused by a chill on the nerves.

My brother's Bill and Davie, had to go back to school without me. The blisters were very tender, particularly when they burst. I couldn't bear to be touched on the back, even through thick clothing.

After Easter, the soup kitchen was closed until the winter months, so we had to bring packed lunches. There wasn't ready made sandwich filling, or ready sliced bread, in those days. However, thickly cut bread, with butter, home made jam, or cheese, or eggs, washed down with cold tea, brought in a glass, screw top bottle, seemed a treat to us. At least we could avoid the school's soup.

Sometimes we had money to buy something extra from the grocer's cart, as a treat. Mainly we just enjoyed getting away from the frequent fights in the playground, and enjoyed watching the abundant wildlife around us.

The Squirrel

*A*s we ate our packed lunch we would watch the bees visiting the flowers, or study the caterpillars. We were fascinated by the way they moved, stretching out flat then pulling the middle of their body up into a hump then stretching out flat again. They seemed comical to us, and if we picked them up to watch their peculiar way of moving across our palms, they tickled.

Early in the Spring there seemed to be hundreds of little red spiders, which grew very quickly. We used to watch their progress and see how they spun their webs. There was a variety of different kinds of spiders and other insects. We were interested in everything that moved.

I took longer than usual to eat my sandwiches one day, mainly because I was feeding crumbs to the birds. I was sitting quietly on my own when I noticed an unusual animal, some distance away. I hadn't seen one of these small, red, furry creatures before. It was a red squirrel, which was digging up its winter store of nuts.

It was concentrating on scraping away furiously at the ground, so it didn't notice me walk quietly up to it.

I looked down at the soft, russet coat, not noticing the sharp claws or teeth. I tried to stroke the squirrel. As soon as I touched it, the squirrel moved at an amazing speed. It turned round, bit my finger to the bone, turned back, grabbed a nut in its mouth, raced for a nearby tree, and sat watching my brothers when they came to my aid.

It sat there staring at us and eating the nut, while Bill tried to stem the flow of blood. I felt as if it was mocking us, but probably it was afraid of us. In a few days the cut had healed, but I knew not to get too close to a squirrel again.

The squirrel wasn't the only creature to bite me. Once, when I replaced a stone on the dyke at the foot of our garden, I had quite a surprise when a mouse popped out from under the stone. It bit me on the finger and disappeared into the dyke. It moved so quickly that I couldn't believe it happened; or wouldn't have believed it happened if it wasn't for the pain in my finger. I always wore gloves while moving stones, after that experience.

One animal which I learned the hard way to treat with caution, is the ferret. They make interesting pets providing they're kept in an outhouse, as they are rather smelly. If cared-for properly they seem quite happy to live in captivity. One of my older brothers had a ferret, which was sometimes used for rabbit hunting so it was almost a wild creature. Being not only interested in animals, but nosey as well, I watched my brother cut liver into strips to feed his hungry ferret. The ferret ran excitedly back and fore in the hutch, while my brother went off to wash the blood off his hands.

I started to feed the hungry ferret by pushing strips of liver through the wire mesh. The ferret grabbed the first strip, ran to the other end of the hutch, and returned very quickly for a second piece. The second strip of liver was swallowed even quicker than the first, and the third piece grabbed with amazing speed. Unfortunately, it bit my finger, which was covered in liver blood, and it wouldn't let go.

My brother Donald heard my screams from the house and guessed what had happened. He ran from the house with a box of matches. He struck a match and held it under the ferret's nose. The ferret let go without having the tip of my finger for its dinner. Luckily my finger healed quickly, so the only long term effects are a strong dislike, and fear of ferrets.

All wildlife interested us during these school lunch breaks. Sometimes it was insects and at other times it was animals or birds. We would try and get close to birds' nests to see the chicks, and how quickly they were growing. The dinner break never seemed to be long enough, unless it was raining.

Red squirrel

Schoolchildren, c. 1920

The Wild Colts

I enjoyed the long walk to school during the Springtime, with something new to see almost every day. In particular, I loved watching the flocks of migrating birds. Some of the birds were leaving, others were arriving and some seemed to call in on their way to somewhere else. There were unusual birds, which we only seemed to see at this time of the year, if we were lucky. If we passed near a flock resting in a field, they would all rise up in the air as one. The noise of a great number of wings beating furiously on take off fascinated me.

It was during that first Spring that I first noticed the gurgling of an invisible burn. I ran about looking for the burn, with a couple of equally curious lassies from a nearby farm. We followed the sound for quite a distance, over the moor towards the hill; then Bill came looking for us and explained that it was an underground burn, which we would never find. We looked for it a few times in fine weather, but never did find the source of the burn.

One morning, on our way to school, I saw horses in the distance, grazing on the moor. Bill warned us to walk quietly and quickly across the moor, "Don't make any sudden movements, don't hang about or even stare at these young horses. Don't even speak. Those horses are unbroken colts, temperamental and dangerous."

On the way back I found out what he meant. We were crossing the moor and were about half way between the gates when one of the colts saw us. We didn't seem to be in danger from the colt, but these young unbroken horses were not used to people. Although they were not fully grown, they were workhorses. They seemed to be Clydesdales, one of the larger breeds of shire horses, which grow to about eighteen hands. They were as excitable as small ponies, but they were already large and heavy. Some were almost fully grown.

The colt watched us for a few seconds and seemed disinterested. Then suddenly it was galloping towards us, followed by the others. "Run!" shouted Bill, but I was already running. The loud neighing, and the sight of these crazy colts, and fillies alarmed me. I was already running towards the gate. The gate seemed miles away and I thought my heart would burst with fear, and the effort of trying to get there in time. I could hear their massive hooves pounding the ground behind me. How could we get over the high five bar gate?

The horses were almost on us. Bill must have grabbed me, as I felt as if I flew the last few yards. Somehow we were all over the gate safely, although I couldn't remember how we got there. A large wild eyed colt was reaching over the gate, trying to bite us. He was so close that I could feel his damp, hot breath on my face.

I used to have nightmares of these massive black horses, with their white faces and dark menacing eyes. They would chase me all night long. They would eventually catch up with me and trample me into the ground.

That first chase nearly ended in tragedy. We always ran for the nearest part of the dry-stane dyke, after that incident. That was also dangerous, as we chanced pulling large, sharp stones down on ourselves. These unbroken young horses were less excitable on our way to school in the mornings. They always seemed to be grazing farther away, on high ground. They either ignored us, or were unaware of our presence. We were able to avoid a long detour, which would have made us late for school.

The afternoons were different. If one horse decided to chase anyone crossing the moor, then they all joined in the mad dash. This happened several times a week, for several weeks of the year, every year; then they became less skittish, and the attacks became less frequent, and less ferocious.

The colts also seemed to be affected by the weather and their surroundings. If heavy rain or a thunderstorm was due, they huddled together at the far side of the moor and didn't bother anyone. In late Spring, in hot weather, they didn't have the energy to chase people. At other times, the sudden movement of a hawk swooping on prey, or of an animal nearby, panicked them. They would scatter across the moor and were more likely to chase people crossing the moor. Quite a few people used the right of way over the moor, including the postman on his daily deliveries. I couldn't understand why the farmer, who owned the horses, put our lives in danger year after year. Did no one at that time question his right to act in such a reckless and uncaring way? I wonder now, if he watched us from a distance enjoying the spectacle.

Fortunately, there always seems to be more caring, thoughtful, people about than there are hard hearted types. During this time of the year when I feared crossing the moor, and had nightmares about being trampled, kicked and bitten by colts, I saw one farm-worker who was soft hearted.

I stopped for a minute or two to watch a farm-worker roll a field with a heavy, horse drawn roller. When he came to birds nests, he lifted them out of the path of the roller; then carefully replaced them afterwards. Obviously, he didn't work for the owner of the colts.

There was more to interest and delight us on our route to and from school, than there was to endanger or worry us, such as wild flowers. The first snowdrops in the midst of early greenery, trees in bud, or banks of wild deep yellow primroses, would fill me full of joy and lighten my steps as I went on my way.

The Crystal Set

The school closed for the school holidays in an air of excitement. We played beside the frog pool for longer than usual, as we would not be back for months.

During the holiday we spent some time in Inverurie, where I made friends with a five year old girl. She had long, dark ringlets and a friendly smile. We were playing on the swings when her father came for her. "Come and listen to the crystal set", he said, taking her by the hand. "What's a crystal set?" I asked my friend. Her father answered. "Come and see for yourself. You'll be able to hear people speaking from London."

I told Davie where we were going, and went to their house on The Square. I didn't know where London was, but I knew it was a long way away. This made me curious enough to venture into a strange house, but I was not disappointed. I listened through the headphones and was amazed how clear the voices were. They were much clearer than our old phonograph, but unlike a telephone there was no wire. I could understand how a telephone worked, as you can hear sounds travelling along a wire without the use of a handset. Without wires this seemed marvellous.

Donald and Tommy came looking for me as they were afraid I was lost in a strange town. The man let them hear the crystal set too. They thought it was marvellous. We rushed home to tell our parents about "The Marvellous Crystal Set". Although my parents had heard about crystal sets, they had never listened to one. I was the first in my family to experience the wireless, yet by the time I was fourteen years old we had a more modern, battery powered wireless set.

A few months after my experience with the Crystal set, a relative gave Bill an old crystal set which he was throwing out. Unlike the set in Inverurie the signal was very poor. This set only seemed to pick up a few crackles and whispers. My brothers tried the set out in different parts of the house, and in different areas outside. They also tried fiddling with it, but it was no use and they gave up in the end. We didn't try a new set as we thought they didn't work in our area. None of us realized, at the time, that the power in the crystal gets used up. Just like a battery, it eventually has to be replaced.

I can't imagine an invention today which would have enough impact on people, that they would invite strangers into their home to experience it. The crystal sets were advertised by using a rhyme, which became popular with children:

Father bought a "Crystal Set,"
the very best that he could get.

Every evening after tea,
baby, brother, sister and me
put receivers on our head,
and listen till we go to bed.

A year later, during the school holiday, I saw a silent film for the first time. It was a Charlie Chaplin film about skaters. Eight years later I saw my first real talking film, while visiting relatives in Aberdeen. It was "The Sign Of The Cross" a very moving film, which I still remember in every detail. Along with it was "Gene Autry, The Singing Cowboy". For a short time I was a frequent visitor to the cinema, surrounded by my younger brothers, sisters and cousins.

It was about five years later that I saw a film in colour for the first time. I was in Edinburgh, during the war. Then I saw that great film "Gone With The Wind" in Peterhead about 1944. It had a great impact on audiences, at a time when most people didn't even have electric lights in their homes.

The improvement in wireless and films, in just a few years is amazing. However, to me in 1926, experiencing "The Crystal Set" was wonderful, a truly exciting moment for a six year old.

Rabbit Hunting

*A*t weekends, evenings and holidays, my brothers would go out hunting for rabbits. Sometimes I would go with them, as I always wanted to join in everything they did.

Their main method of hunting, was to let the dogs do practically all the work. We always had two whippets which were fast, agile and graceful. Although I didn't like seeing the dogs go in for the kill, they are beautiful to watch, and the rabbits are dispatched in a split second. It's a humane way to hunt, unlike using traps which can inflict hours of pain on the trapped animal.

My brothers didn't hunt rabbits when they were rearing young. It's cruel and eventually there would have been few rabbits in our area to hunt. They don't taste so good at that time of the year anyway. Some of the farmers shot rabbits, but my Father didn't approve of guns. He'd seen gunshot wounds in the First World War and, as a medic, was well aware of the pain and damage guns can inflict. He also disapproved of keeping guns in a household where there were children, as accidents can happen even in careful households.

Shooting rabbits can be expensive and wasteful. Even an expert shot can hit a small creature like a rabbit on the body, which ruins it by making such a mess of the body that there's hardly any meat left on it worth eating. The damage to the pelt makes that worthless too.

Sometimes, a ferret would be used, along with the dogs. One of my brothers would carry his ferret in a small, wooden hutch; which was strapped to his back. When a rabbit warren currently in use was chosen, all but two of the entrances were blocked. The ferret, keen to get at a rabbit, was released into one of the holes. Any rabbits in the warren would have to try and escape through the only remaining exit. The two whippets would wait for the escaping rabbits. If one rabbit came out, one of the whippets would grab it by the head, killing it instantly. If two rabbits came out, each dog would grab one. If more than two came out they usually got away; although, sometimes, the whippets were so quick they could catch another one.

The ferret would follow the rabbits out of the hole. It would have to be grabbed quickly, by the back of the neck, and replaced in its box. If there were a few rabbits, we were unlikely to see the ferret for a while. The ferret would catch a rabbit, eat it, then fall asleep. My brothers would stay there, whistling, and calling for the ferret, making as much noise as possible. Sometimes, they would wait there for hours before they got the ferret back.

Nora, one of our whippets, always seemed to be very impatient as she waited for the rabbits to be driven out. One day she was repeatedly called back from the hole, but she kept running back and sticking her nose into the hole. The ferret shot out of the hole, and sank its teeth into the whippets nose. As ferrets are afraid of dogs, it hung on, digging its teeth deeper into Nora's nose.

Nora was in a great deal of pain. She tried to shake the ferret off, in vain. The ferret managed to hang on, even after Nora repeatedly smashed her own head against a boulder. I was sure the ferret was going to bite our dog's noise off.

One of my brothers grabbed the whippet by the collar. Another brother grabbed the ferret by the back of the neck, and put a dead rabbit to its nose. The ferret tried to transfer its grip to the rabbit, and was quickly returned to its mobile home. If it had managed to get hold of the rabbit, it would have been very difficult to get it back into the box. The ferret had to wait until it was back home in the large hutch before it had rabbit to eat.

Nora recovered from the ferret's attack, and even resumed hunting with my brothers. However, she always stayed well back from the rabbit warrens when the ferret was released into the warren. She preferred to wait, and make sure it was a rabbit before chasing it. She always came back with a rabbit, even when she had to chase it for a long distance. She was also very nervous whenever the ferret was near.

A friend of my father used a dog to hunt rabbits. One day, his dog chased a rabbit in to a dry conduit, under a road. The dog seemed to be stuck in the conduit. The dog's owner couldn't reach the dog, so he crossed the road to the other end of the drain, and called his dog. The dog had caught hold of the rabbit. When his master called, he barked, releasing the rabbit. The rabbit shot out of the conduit, causing a head on collision with the man.

When the man regained consciousness, he had a severe headache, a large lump on his forehead, and a dead rabbit for the pot. The dog reversed out of the conduit, unharmed.

We hunted rabbits for the pot, but a good pelt was worth sixpence. At that time, a large loaf of bread cost two and a half pence. By today's values, a pelt would be worth about £1.50. Some hunters sold rabbits to butchers, where they would be sold for about a shilling (5 pence).

I used to feel sorry for the rabbits. They were being shot at, snared, and hunted by dogs, ferrets, eagles and weasels. I felt that they didn't have much of a life.

Ferret

My Second and Third
Year at School

When I returned to school after my first Summer holiday, the newness and anticipation that I felt during that first year were gone. Some events stand out, but it is not always possible to say which year they happened in. School carried on much the same as before and our main interest, which was the local wildlife, continued to interest us. After so many years it all merges into a pattern. I can think myself back to particular events and places and my memory is so clear that I feel I am actually there, but time and dates mean little to these memories. I think of the first and second years as one period of time. The greatest change at school was the introduction of new children to our area, who were strangers to life in the countryside.

During the second or third year, orphans were boarded out to people in our area. We were told they weren't really "Home

Bairns". They were children who had lost their fathers' in "The Great War". Some of these children would eventually be going home to their mothers or other relatives. They didn't wear the usual rough grey material, which reminded people of the old workhouses or orphanages. My mother never dressed us in grey. She said grey was for clergymen and "Home Bairns". We were told not to call these children orphans, they were called "Boarded-out Children".

The school was so crowded now that fourteen children in my age group were sent through to the headmaster's classroom, for a while, to make room for the extra children.

Miss Gill chose a section of the class to go, but allowed us to swap places. Children like me, who particularly wanted to go, were allowed to swap places with those children who were chosen, but wanted to stay. Some children didn't want to be separated from their friends, or were afraid of the bigger pupils. I wanted to go because I wanted to learn History and Geography.

When we were transferred to the headmaster's classroom, we were not actually part of his class. Two clever lassies were given the task of teaching us. They were clever enough to keep up with their own lessons, and still found time to take it in turn teaching us. I learned more under their tuition, than with any of the teachers we had.

We all tried to please these lassies, as they were pleasant lassies who were already popular with the younger pupils. We also had more individual tuition, as we were a small group. This encouraged us all to do better.

I loved being in the headmaster's classroom. I would hurry

through the work set for us, so that I could listen to the lessons that the headmaster was giving to the older classes. Our headmaster made the lessons interesting. My favourite lessons were stories of "British Explorers." I can still remember the headmaster telling us about "The Adventures Of Captain Cook." My vivid imagination, and the headmaster's skill in telling these stories, brought "Captain Cook's Adventures" to life.

When we moved to the headmaster's classroom, Sandy Duncan sat beside me. He wanted to be with two of his cousins, who were chosen to be transferred. We became particularly good friends. Although we were the same age, Sandy was even smaller than me. Sandy had a hare lip and some of the older children made fun of him. I accepted Sandy the way he was, but when the older children made fun of him I told them to "Lay off, leave Sandy alone."

These older children weren't going to pick on me because I had two older brothers at school. The other children of our age then supported Sandy when they saw me getting away with it. Sandy was good natured, with a good sense of humour and was well liked by the other children of our age.

I think we must have been in the headmaster's class for over a year. My brother Andy started school while I was there, but I was eventually moved back to join him. The rest of my age group started ink exercises and I was anxious to move back as I was afraid we would be left behind. Writing with ink wasn't quite so easy as using a fountain pen, or ballpoint pen. We wrote with a wooden pen and nib, which we dipped in ink. It could be quite messy until you got the hang of it.

Shortly after the ink exercises started, our group was exchanged for another group, so we were able to catch up. The school was always overcrowded by then. It had been built as a school for the "Finzean Estate", when there was a smaller population, a long time before. There was nowhere else for the children to go and the boarded-out children added to the overcrowding. People seemed to feel sorry for the boarded-out children, but when we saw their books and found out that they were being supplied with everything the school requested, then they didn't seem so badly off to us. Few of the other children had full sets of new text books and jotters. I have known children who, when they came to the end of a text book, erased all the old writing with a rubber and started again, over and over again until the jotter fell apart.

The number of boarded-out children varied a lot. Sometimes children went home, or to other relatives, then new children replaced them. Sometimes there were so many new children that extra places were found for them, in the Finzean area. Now that children were coming and going all the time, I don't know how our teacher coped.

These extra children caused trouble with the local children, as they were more likely to complain. If they complained to the people they were lodged with, a letter was sent to the school. The complaint was upheld, without being properly investigated, and the punishment was the strap. Some of these complaints were bound to be unfair. I found to my own cost that it was better to stay away from these children.

One little girl was thought to be comical when her skirt got caught up in her knickers while she was in the toilet. I tried to help her by freeing her skirt and was reported for making fun of her. I was angry with the child for getting me the strap, as I was only trying to help her. These children became very unpopular with the rest of the school, along with any children who spoke to them.

Some of these extra children seemed to have odd ideas about the countryside. One memory that sticks with me is the time our teacher, during an art class, asked one of these city laddies to describe the colours of the nearby hills. He sat in silence, looking out of the window at the hills. "Joseph, what colours are you looking at on the hills." Joseph looked unsure of himself for a moment, then he proudly replied, "Tartan, Miss."

Pigeons

One of my brothers made a small doo'cot (dovecot) and laid out a trail of our horse's corn, to entice pigeons to nest there. Soon there was three doo'cots, all the handiwork of three of my older brothers. Each thought that his doo'cot was the best, and his pigeons were the best. Although this was just a hobby with my brothers, the pigeons laid too many eggs for the size of their loft so when there were a lot of spare eggs, we just ate them. Pigeons' eggs are tiny but delicious. At one time they were considered a delicacy by the landed gentry in Scotland. In the 15th and 16th century dovecots were an essential part of a castle. Harming a laird's pigeons could result in a beating or instant execution.

Racing pigeons joined the wild variety when a racing pigeon fancier gave my brothers some of his birds eggs, telling them to get their hens to hatch the eggs.

I loved to see the racing pigeons fly, as they flew to a great height and circled round and round, gradually getting farther away. They could be away for hours, but they always came back.

Neeps

All this exercise gave us healthy appetites. One of my friends from one of the nearer farms also had a good appetite. I watched her one day pulling small turnips from her father's field, and eat them raw as a snack. She pulled off the leafy green parts and smashed them against a stone, to get at the tender insides. She invited us to help ourselves as they were about to be thinned out. A lot of these little neeps would be left to rot. I didn't need to be asked a second time as I was always ready to eat, and assumed that if she told me to do it, that it would be O.K.

We might have got away with this, but we pulled up the larger turnips at the end of the drills. Her father was not pleased. He was not nice natured at any time. I think the only time I ever saw him laugh was when I tripped over a lump of frozen mud and fell, skinning my knees. Before I had a chance to get up, he asked if I was taking a rest. I didn't think it was funny at the time.

This time he shouted at us, calling us thieves and not to do it again. Although his daughter was really to blame, and told him this, he went to my father and complained about us. Father was very embarrassed about this and agreed that it was theft. We didn't touch any farmer's vegetables after that.

At the time I was sorry for my friend, not angry at her for the trouble she caused us. I was just glad that my father was not a mean, miserable man, like her father.

My First Concert

I didn't take part in the concert during the second year, as I was still considered to too be young to be out in the evening during the winter. During the third year, when I was eight years old, I was chosen to sing in the concert. The song I remember best is "Soldier Soldier". The lassies sang "Oh soldier, soldier, will you marry me? etc." Then the laddies sang the reply. To encourage us to learn the whole song, Miss Gill didn't tell us the punch line until we knew all the other verses of the song. We were all eager to find out the punch line and as we had to wait until just before the concert to get the whole story, the song was still fresh when we sang it in front of an audience.

I thoroughly enjoyed singing in the school concert in front of an audience and was very proud to be chosen to sing in all of the girls choruses. There were also several soloists. I felt that the best singer was Bessie, one of the boarded-out lassies, who was an outstanding singer. The audience seemed to agree with me, judging by the applause she received. My parents enjoyed the concert and were proud of our efforts.

After that school concert, I took part in every school concert until I left. The concerts seemed to give quieter children confidence. When my sister Margaret, who was five years younger than me, started school she was very shy. She started school with our niece Mary, who was the same age and lived near us. Both Margaret and Mary were shy. When the teacher spoke to them, they held their heads down and whispered an answer. They did everything together and reacted to everything the same way, both Margaret and Mary were withdrawn and reluctant to speak to anyone, yet they took part in a concert in their first year at school. Although we had a different teacher then, she still managed to get them to go on the stage. Seven little girls, including Margaret and Mary, took part in a song called "Seven Little Cherubs". They wore white nightdresses and carried candles on white ceramic, "Wee Willie Winkie" candle holders. Mother was so proud of them that she bought both girls beautiful new nightdresses for their stage appearance. They sang on the front row with another little girl, and four older lassies in white nighties and candles singing behind them. The end of the song was "Blew out the candles and said goodnight". They brought a tear to the eyes of some of our audience, and I could hardly believe that they'd done so well. The smiles on their faces showed that they would never be quite so shy again.

Immediately after the concert there was a fund raising sale. More raffle tickets were sold and the draw was made later in the evening. There was a home bakes stall with toffee made by the older lassies. A craft-work stall and also a sales stall of other things which were handed in. Some of the funds raised provided bus-runs and picnics for Finzean schoolchildren during the summer holidays. We were always away during the summer holidays, so we never went on any of the outings.

During my second year at school, the only change during the festive season, was the time of "The Laird's Christmas Party". It was changed to the evening and we had to be met by an adult. The party was just as good as before, but my sister Mary picked us up in the gig. The laird told us all to wait in the ballroom until we were collected. It always seemed to be a fine frosty evening for our trip home. Everything seemed to sparkle in the moonlight, as if the shimmering light from the Christmas tree had followed us outside. The frost always made the journey home seem special, almost magical. We couldn't wait to get home with our cakes, fruit and gifts. We also talked non-stop to Mary, all the way home, giving her a detailed description of everything that had interested us that evening.

My gift on the second year was a sweet shop, with jars of sweets, bags, real scales and a till. We played with it for years and replaced the sweets in the jars, when we had pocket money. The following year I received a book which told a fairy story and also had a pantomime script for us to act out the story. We made our own costumes and had great fun putting on our own pantomime, despite never having been to a real pantomime. I know all my brothers and sisters who were lucky enough to attend these Christmas parties thoroughly enjoyed them. In summer, the laird also supplied the ground for the school sports.

The Finzean school sports day was part of an open sports competition, which was almost a mini highland games. There were bagpipe competitions for juniors and also adults, if any wanted to compete. There was highland dancing competitions, which I really enjoyed and there were also adults competing in sports, including ladies' races. This was probably unusual in those days. The prize money was good for the junior races. I thought I had a chance of coming in among the first three, and earning some pocket money.

The long journey to and from school made it necessary for us to run a good part of the way, which gave us ample running practice. I imagined that this would help me win the race. When the whistle blew I thought I shot off at a great speed, but several older, long legged lassies passed me as if I were still standing. I found the stamina we built up on these journeys was good for endurance, not speed. Tall thin people usually make better sprinters. I still enjoyed our school sports day, even without winning any prizes.

The remainder of the second and third years were much the same as any other school year and our main interests were in the wildlife in the countryside around us and making friends with children who shared part of our walk to and from school.

The Gander

After our close shave in the fierce storm, my father bought me a long, red, knitted scarf, to match my coat. It was a long scarf, long enough to wrap round my neck and if needed, also wrap over my hat; keeping me warm in the coldest weather. I normally wore it wrapped twice round my neck with quite a long end of scarf hanging over my shoulder and down my back. I loved the way it flew out at the back when I ran, but I had good reason to stop that habit, after a frightening experience I had with a gander.

Muggie and Alick's father kept geese and hens in a copse which we walked past on our way to and from school. This didn't normally present us with any problems, but in Spring the geese tend to become very excitable. Possibly it was because they had just started laying eggs and the Spring grass was coming through, which they tended to fight over. Geese eat a lot of grass, preferring the new tender shoots. They can also be frightening if disturbed at any time of the year, making excellent watchdogs.

It must have been the month of April, in my second or third school year, when I was chased by the gander.

We were coming home from school with Muggie and Alick, when we realised the geese were making more noise than usual. My brothers warned me to walk slowly past. "Whatever you do don't run. They'll try and make you run but don't run, if you do they'll chase you. Ignore them!" I was already nervous, when some of the geese left the wood and came running at us, flapping their wings and calling loudly. I quickened my pace slightly, getting a little ahead of my brothers so the gander singled me out for attention. It ran at me flapping its wings and making a threatening sucking and hissing sound, which frightened me. When its wing brushed against my leg, I was off and running like a frightened rabbit. In my state of panic I actually thought that I could outrun a gander.

The gander took off after me. I could feel the force of the air from its wings on my back, and thought it was going to land on me. Suddenly there was a great weight on the end of my scarf, which jerked the scarf tight and I was choking. The gander had stopped my mad dash, but its weight on the end of my scarf was still choking me. I tore at my scarf, trying to loosen it while gasping for breath. Bill and Davie started pulling at the rest of the scarf, trying to unwind it, but for a few seconds I felt as if the scarf was being pulled tighter. The gander would not let go. Alick tried to pick it up to lessen the weight and tried to hold the gander still, but it fought him and all he could get hold of was the gander's leg which he tried to keep hold of, while worrying about injuring his father's gander. The rest of the geese came to the aid of the old gander. We seemed to be surrounded by noisy, attacking geese, beating us with their wings while hissing and pecking us. Then the scarf was off and my brothers were trying to pull my scarf from the gander.

In a daze I watched the mad tug of war. My brothers held on to the scarf, which stretched, threatening to tear. Muggie grabbed the scarf nearer the gander and Alick got hold of the gander trying to force it to let go of the scarf, risking being pecked by the gander. Davie solved the situation by winding the scarf round the gander. "Have the scarf then, see how you like it round your neck." This seemed to panic the old gander, which suddenly wanted to be free of the scarf and was soon flying off with a beak full of red woollen fringe, leaving me with a scarf which was now twice the length.

My lovely, soft woollen scarf was now like a hard rope. I still wore it for ages afterwards but not with a length of scarf flying out behind me when I ran. I now had to wrap it round my neck and head so many times, it looked like I was wearing a collapsed turban. My brothers always reminded me about the incident by saying, "Chrissie, dae you mind aboot 'Goosie, Goosie, Gander'?"

Andy's First Year

When my brother Andy started school Bill and Davie were in the headmaster's class and I was still with a temporary class in the headmaster's classroom, but I should have been taking Andy home as we should have left school together. The headmaster tended to forget that we should leave with the others from the teacher's class. None of us liked to remind the headmaster that it was time for us to go. I worried about Andy going home alone, and told him to wait for me, but Andy wanted to walk part of the way with a girl from his group and her older sister.

The sisters were not at all alike. The five year old was tiny and liked Andy. She was a pleasant natured lassie, a bit of a chatter-box and was well liked by the other young children. Her older sister was about my age, but was tall and thin. I didn't like her as she was sullen, argumentative and seemed to have a permanent bubble attached to one nostril. She never seemed to blow her nose but was frequently sniffing the bubble up, which only reappeared a minute or two later. The same bubble seemed to travel up and down her nose all day.

The sight and sound of this bubble being sniffed up made me feel sick. She was a rather odd lassie and I didn't trust her to look after my brother, in fact I didn't trust anyone other than my older brothers to look after Andy. Andy was only six years old at the time and was still very vulnerable. I told Andy to wait for me when I was late, but he wouldn't wait. One day when we were even later than usual getting out of the headmaster's classroom, I ran out of school and up the hill after Andy, in the hope of catching up with him before Sniffy picked on him. Before long I could see Andy and the sisters in the distance and Andy was already in trouble.

Big Sniffy hit him with her leather satchel and as he backed away she swung the satchel at him again and again. The little sister seemed to be trying to stop her and even went between Sniffy and Andy. Sniffy turned on her little sister and swung the heavy bag into her face. By the time I arrived she was swinging the bag in turn at both Andy and her little sister.

Grabbing the bag from her, I threw it in a nearby ditch and went to the aid of her little sister and Andy. I tried to find out what had started the argument, while Sniffy removed her bag from the ditch. Unfortunately for me, just as I grabbed the satchel, a ploughman in one of their father's fields came up over a rise in the field he was ploughing and saw me. He went over to Andy while I tried to get the little sister, who's nose was bleeding and face red and swollen, to tell me what had happened. The ploughman, who was a young, unusually large man, hadn't seen what went on before I grabbed the satchel. He had the wrong idea when he spoke to Andy.

He said to Andy. "Shall I hit her loon? Shall I hit her?"

Andy, thinking that the ploughman meant Sniffy said "Aye."

I wasn't paying attention to the ploughman, when a powerful blow to the side of my head burst my ear drum and lifted me off my feet, depositing me, unconscious, in the ditch. Before I came round I heard Andy repeatedly shouting my name, as if he was far away. Then I felt him shaking me, shouting "You're nae deid! You're nae deid! Tell me you're nae deid!"

When I came round Andy hauled me out of the ditch. I was hardly able to walk at first, but eventually we made it home. I told Andy to say nothing about what had happened, as any time we complained about being bullied at school my mother would not believe us. She always accused us of starting the trouble and I felt that Mother's attitude made the pain feel worse. I felt too ill to put up with a fuss anyway. If I complained to my father, under the circumstances he might go to the ploughman and demand an explanation. The man was young and massive. If he hit me then I didn't think he would mind hitting a little middle aged man. Father could end up seriously injured, or even dead. I wouldn't even tell Bill or Davie, when they caught up with us on the way home.

As the side of my face was red, swollen and becoming bruised, it was obvious that I had been in some sort of accident or incident, but I refused to tell my parents what had happened. Next day at school the story of how I had beaten up Andy's little friend and thrown Sniffy's bag in the ditch was there before me

The ploughman was actually pleased with himself and had been telling everyone around about how he had sorted out a bully. The only people in our area that didn't get the story wrong were my parents, who knew nothing about either the incident or his boasting. To make matters worse Andy decided to blackmail me, threatening to tell Father what really happened.

Andy tried blackmailing me to do something for him, when I was already doing something for Mother. Father overheard him and demanded to hear the whole story. My father was furious and went over to see the sister's father right away. He asked the sister's father to question his younger daughter, who was too frightened of her older sister and the ploughman to speak up and tell the truth. She told her father the real story. Her father was very apologetic, saying that he didn't want anyone like that working for him.

"I would sack him, but he's already leaving. I might as well let him work his time oot. He's been accepted by the police force."

This news made me feel even worse. Now that the truth was out the ploughman might blame me for telling my father about him. He might attack me again before he left. He might lie in wait for me on the way home from school. I prayed desperately every night to God to protect me from this man. After he left, I feared that I would meet him at some time in the future, that he would have the advantage of being a policeman and perhaps be outside of the law. I continued praying to God for protection, for the next two or three years; then I heard that he'd died of pneumonia.

When I heard of his death I actually felt guilty. Although I had prayed only for protection, I was bitter about the incident. I felt it was unfair that he should get away with his attack on me, I wished that he had been punished. When he died I felt as if I had contributed in some way to his death, but I was only a child of eight years at the time of the incident, and had good reason to feel bitter.

After the incident I felt that something had to be done, as Sniffy might take some sort of revenge on Andy. I told Andy to knock on the door of the headmaster's classroom when he got out of school, and ask if his sister's class was due out yet. When he did this the headmaster seemed pleased that someone had reminded him to let the junior class out on time. It's a pity I didn't think of this before the incident; it would have saved me from worry, pain and fear. It would also have saved me from about seventy years of having a false story told about me.

Bill's Invention

During my third year at school, I became more effective at fighting off bullies. My brother Davie, two years older than me, could only stick up for himself until he was hit on the nose. The slightest blow on the nose brought the blood flowing, which the bullies were quick to take advantage of. On one occasion a lad of about the same age, but taller with a much longer reach, picked a fight with Davie. Davie managed to fight him off, while keeping his head back, until the other boy picked up a handful of snow, which he would have rubbed in Davie's face.

I imagined Davie with blood pouring down his face and jacket, as it had done on previous occasions. I could see Davie becoming a regular victim of bullies, frequently picked on, perhaps even afraid to go to school. I felt I had to do something.

Quickly I picked up a snowball in haste and before realising it was a lump of ice, formed by pressure in the hollow of a horses hoof, I hurled the ice at the big laddie, hitting him on the side of the head just before Davie landed a punch on the same place. The big laddie staggered about, weak at the knees and complained of feeling sick. He already had a colourful bruise beside his eye, which was growing larger and more colourful by the minute. Everyone, including Davie, thought it was the result of Davie's punch. My brother Andy put him right about that, on the way home. "You'd better nae start imagining you can punch like that Davie, or the biggest loons will soon realise you're a softie and you'll have to fight them before long." None of the other children found out the truth about Davie's powerful punch and none of them picked a fight with him again.

The fight came about because Bill was not around at the time. Everyone liked my brother Bill. I never saw him involved in a fight at school, and no one picked on us if he was nearby. Minutes later he appeared with a catapult he'd invented. The catapult had a wooden base on which Bill had cut a groove, so it could be sighted like a gun. The trigger was a springy, steel, corset stay, attached at one end of the base. Bill had already tried it out on nearby trees, to see if it worked. Now he was ready to demonstrate his invention.

At the sight of the strange looking weapon, all the pupils gathered round to see what Bill was going to do. He aimed his catapult at the weather vane on the school roof, to see how close he could fire it. Using a small stone as ammunition, he took careful aim. Silence fell over the playground and I held my breath in anticipation. Bill's aim was perfect and his catapult was powerful enough to knock the beak off the cockerel on the weather vane with one shot.

A great cheer went up from the playground. I thought Bill was going to disappear under a pile of laddies, all keen to see his marvellous catapult, or just congratulate him. The headmaster came out to see what was going on, but no one admitted that anything had happened. He didn't seem to notice any damage, but if he had it's doubtful that he would have strapped Bill. Bill was always so polite, so apologetic and rarely did anything wrong; so when he did do something wrong, he usually got away with it.

Bill made several catapults, which my brothers tried out while hunting rabbits. The catapults were hidden inside their coats, as I don't think my father would have been very pleased to catch them with these weapons. After a time they went back to hunting with the dogs, which were sometimes aided by a ferret.

Eventually they lost interest in the catapult, or ran out of corset stays, and Bill went on to make other things, none of which had such a dramatic demonstration as the day Bill shot the beak off the weather vane cockerel.

My Little Friend

While we were going to school at the beginning of the school year, when I was a bit older, a farmer at one of the nearer farms we passed through called me over. His little girl, who was his eldest child, was starting school that day. Her father was concerned at her starting on her own, and asked me to take her to school with us. I was proud to be trusted with his daughter's safety and cared for her as if she was one of my sisters. I introduced her to our school's dry toilets at break time, but I warned her not to look into the hole. She was so small that she had to be lifted onto the seat at first, but I assured her that the hole wasn't as big as it looked. I also introduced her to the nicer, younger girls, who I knew wouldn't bully her. She was a cheerful, friendly lassie and quickly made friends at school. Soon she joined a group of younger lassies for most of the journey to and from school.

My little friend's parents were a nice couple, and appreciated the help I gave their daughter. We didn't have much contact with the local farmers as my parents told us to stay out of their way. This family was an exception and were liked and respected by my parents.

On one occasion when I was walking through their farmyard with Andy, a large sow came running towards us. The farmer shouted to us to block his sow's way and try and turn her back. The sow turned to run back, but seeing the farmer ahead she just stopped where she was. Shouting didn't encourage the sow to move so he told us to hit his pig on the rear. He probably meant us to look for a stick to tap her with. Without thinking, we both slapped the pig on the rear, but neither the slap or our howls of pain encouraged her to move one inch.

Slapping the pig was like hitting a roughcast wall. "Why did you not just tell us tae pick a fight wae a dyke?" I asked with tears in my eyes. He was very apologetic and told us to go into the house and his wife would give us a cup of tea and a scone. Our hands hurt so much we refused, as we felt sick with pain. By the time we got home we could see the funny side of the incident, as our hands were less painful, but we couldn't tell Mother why our hands hurt. Every time we tried to explain, it seemed such a stupid thing to do that we just fell about laughing.

Miss Gill Retires

Miss Gill was probably over seventy years old when I started my schooling at Finzean school. Despite her age she was she was a capable teacher. She kept to a timetable throughout the year, which included hand-crafts, music, cooking and fund-raising. Miss Gill also had control of her pupils, without overuse of the strap, while retaining their respect. Moreover, Miss Gill seemed very healthy as she never seemed to take a day off school. Despite having a raised sole on one boot she was a quick walker, and didn't lack energy. She looked as if she could go on for years, and might have done if she had not suffered an accident on her way to school one morning.

Miss Gill lived in a house on a hill, overlooking the school, which she shared with her sister, who was a talented dressmaker. If we arrived early enough, we could see Miss Gill coming to school in the mornings. From a distance she was unmistakable. She took quick, short steps and wore long, dark dresses. One morning, the path she took to school was muddy causing her to slip and fall, seriously injuring her good ankle. We realised something was wrong when the headmaster rang the handbell in the playground. He came into our class to break the news to us of Miss Gill's accident.

No one knew at that time just how badly Miss Gill's ankle was injured. However, he told us we would get a relief teacher while Miss Gill was away. He left a senior girl in charge while he went home to fetch his wife from his home, which was next to the school. I don't know if the headmaster's wife had ever been a teacher. She seemed to manage well and gave us extra lessons on general knowledge. She was replaced by the first of the relief teachers, who all seemed to be inexperienced young women.

Our lessons resumed under the relief teachers, but we no longer had needle-work, cooking or music lessons. The relief teachers tried their best, but were too inexperienced to control a large class of children of varying ages. The result was increasing use of the belt. The relief teachers usually only stayed for a few weeks. I don't think any of them were educated in country schools and I got the impression that they were all glad to leave our school. Miss Gill returned to teaching, but was obviously in a lot of pain. She couldn't stay on her feet for the whole lesson so she was forced to retire.

When I think of the different age groups and the total control she had over the class, plus her amazing hearing – not a whisper seemed to escape her – then I think she was a wonderful old woman. I didn't fully appreciate Miss Gill at the time, but I liked the way she smiled in approval when we washed our hands after visiting the toilet. There were no towels, and the only tap was an outside, cold-water tap. I appreciated her smile, as although she would tell children to wash their hands on future visits to the toilet, she showed approval when you did wash your hands. She always noticed if a pupil remembered and carried out her instructions, never forgetting to praise them for their efforts, particularly if they did well. She knew all the children and never forgot or muddled our names. When more than one child had the same Christian name, later arrivals were called by both their Christian name and their Sir name. I was unusual, as I was the only Christina in the school.

By the time Miss Gill had her accident the school was very overcrowded. There were always a number of orphans coming and going, but we never referred to them as orphans. They were known as children boarded-out.

When Miss Gill announced her retirement, we contributed to a collection for a gift to remind her of her years at Finzean school. I believe people from far and wide contributed to the fund, as Miss Gill was appreciated and admired for her hand-work and musical ability. She taught at Finzean for many years. I felt that the yearly concert was never quite so good without her.

A year or two after she retired, I called at her house when I was selling raffle tickets for school fund-raising. She bought raffle tickets for a hand made fireside rug, and other prizes. She also entered a name in the doll competition. Miss Gill chose the name Amy, after Amy Johnson the aviator. She advised me not to take too long selling tickets on the way home from school, and to take care of the money I had collected.

Miss Gill had chosen the right name for the doll, and I was proud to have called at her house that day and to have sold her the winning ticket.

I had another pleasant surprise when my name was called out at the draw. There was a prize for the child who sold the most tickets. Although I came second, I sold almost as much as the winner; so they decided to give us both a prize. The prize of two and sixpence, seemed a lot to me. Even better was to follow when my mother showed me my name in *The Press & Journal*, in an article about the "Finzean School Fund-raising Concert".

We had relief teachers for a while after Miss Gill retired. I had good reason to be sorry about Miss Gill's retirement before I was much older.

Another Close Shave

*D*uring late Spring, when I was probably aged nine, we had a long, dry, hot spell which encouraged us to take longer and longer to go home after school. Even the older loons from the farms, who usually rushed home to get on with work about the farm, hung back to play with their pals. The most popular place to gather was the frog pool.

The crowd of bairns at the pool got bigger and we enjoyed ourselves more as the dry spell went on. Children from five years old to thirteen years gathered at the quarry frog pool. Unfortunately we were also getting louder, as the crowd grew larger and children cheered on their chosen frogs. When we gathered at the pool the colts on the moor were always at what seemed to be a safe distance, grazing up the hill.

These massive animals were young and playful. At times they seemed to enjoy chasing people and sometimes they seemed to want to join the children at play. At other times they appeared fierce and we never knew if this was part of their playful high spirits or genuine bad temper. There were too many of them to hang about and find out. They seemed to be either quietly grazing, or galloping as a group. On the day of our close shave, they galloped down the hill towards our group, their approached masked by the noise we were making. Suddenly we were aware of a small herd of "Clydesdale Shire" colts racing towards us. Squeals of laughter turned to screams of terror when we saw these giant horses galloping at us, neighing loudly. We were too far from the first gate to go back; there were too many small children to make for the nearest part of the dry-stane dyke, so we ran along the moor path to the next gate, while the older laddies tried to drive them off.

The older laddies yelled at them and threw stones at the leading colt, which they succeeded in turning back. The big laddies ran after us and had just caught up with us, when the colts turned about and galloped at us again. This time there were no stones on the path. The older laddies, including my brothers, thirteen year old Bill and eleven year old Davie, took their life in their hands and ran between the little bairns and the colts. They shouted and waved their arms, driving them back as we ran for the gate. Then one of the largest colts turned and started kicking its hind legs towards us. This really frightened me as by now they were angry and I knew a hind leg kick is more dangerous than a foreleg kick. If the other colts copied him I could see my brothers, along with the other big laddies, being kicked to death

Fortunately the others didn't join in and as most of the children disappeared through the gate, some of the colts started to lose interest. It was a great relief to see the big laddies come through the gate safely. Some of the children were crying, others laughed nervously, some were quietly shocked by what we children saw as a brush with death.

Later I spoke to my father about the colts. As usual he assured me that shire horses would not harm either adults or children, they are mild natured giants. I felt that they should not be allowed to alarm children, or risk harming them by accident. I kept remembering the big black horse kicking out with its hind legs – their loud neighing, the speed they came at us, and that first fright I had when the colt snapped at me over the gate, its hot breath on the back of my neck before I had even cleared the gate. I still felt that there must be something that could be done to protect the "Right Of Way" route through the moor. However, the colts continued grazing on the moor.

It was years after I left school when the owner of the colts gave up farming in the Finzean area, and the Clydesdale colts stopped grazing on the moor.

Animal Magic

We lived close to nature all year round, as it was just outside our door. Even a short walk to the well could reward you with a glimpse of a fox. We got to know the habits and character of the wildlife around us.

Foxes seemed to me to have deserved the description of "sly as a fox". They would go to ground quickly when they heard anyone approach. A fox is difficult to find once it has gone to ground. If you carry on walking past the place where you last saw it, then turn after a few farther steps, you may catch a glimpse of red hind legs and a bushy tail as it disappears over a dyke.

When we had time to stop in one place and just watch what was going on around us, we were often rewarded by the sight of several animals. The foxes could easily be seen at a distance. When they got used to us they sometimes hunted close by. A fox could be seen stalking its prey from a distance, gradually getting closer. Then it would dart forward for the kill which was over in a split second. Warily, it would make its way home. It stopped now and again to check that it wasn't being followed, then it disappeared into its earth.

There are two kinds of deer in Royal Deeside. The native red deer were quite common when I was a child. They are very timid animals, and can only be seen if you are very quiet and still. They are more likely to be seen in the afternoon or early evening. It is not unusual to see a hind with two calves, which she cares for in an unusual way. She finds a hiding place for one calf among bushes or high heather. She then finds a hiding place for the second calf elsewhere, and goes off to feed on grass and heather. The young deer lie in their hideout perfectly still and almost invisible until their mother returns. The hind will feed herself for a short while, then return to the first calf to allow it to suckle, then she returns to the grassy area to graze for a short time. On the next visit she feeds her second offspring. This goes on throughout the day, every day, until her young ones are less helpless. Their legs will gradually get stronger, until after a few weeks they are able to run from danger.

We got to know the badgers paths and knew when they would be out. They weren't as easily seen as the other animals. However, they are so unusual that they were worth waiting for, especially when there is a family with young badgers walking in a little procession. We never knowingly went near their set, as we didn't want to frighten them away.

One animal which was at one time quite common in the North East of Scotland is the pine marten. Some of our neighbours saw them in nearby woodland, but I never managed to see one. Now and again there would be a sudden movement in a pine tree. For a second I would glimpse a brown shape, then it was gone. Was it a red squirrel, which sometimes appear more brown than red, or was it the larger pine marten, which is now Britain's rarest mammal.

Sometimes we'd look down on the River Dee from a high position, which was almost above the water. The salmon could be seen clearly, swimming in the deep pools. When the weather was hot we would swim in the Dee. I doubt if anyone would recognise the stroke we used, but our swimming was for fun, it was not a serious sport to us. We would wade or swim to an island in the river where a variety of ducks, wild geese, and other birds nested. We didn't touch their nests. We just liked watching every kind of wildlife around us. One bird we kept well away from was the swan. A nesting pair are fearsome if disturbed and are powerful birds. Father warned us to keep well away from them.

There was always plenty of wildlife to see around us, for most of the year. When I look back I always think of the lapwings' song accompanying every scene and I wonder if they can still be found in great numbers around my former childhood home.

Black Bess

*A*lthough I was brought up in a household where there was always contact with a variety of animals I longed for a dog of my own. I was fond of my father's whippets, and I didn't lack the company of children, I just wanted a dog of my own. An elderly relative I had been staying with during part of the school summer holiday one year gave me her dog.

Bess was a black Labrador, a watchdog which had been trained to protect her son's shop. I was overjoyed when my parents decided that I could keep Bess. She was a young, placid, good natured dog. Sometimes I went off for long walks, or would even run with Bess, just for the fun of it. At other times she would join my brothers and the whippets when they were hunting rabbits. It's natural for dogs to hunt, so it didn't take Bess long to join in, and she turned out to be a keen hunter. I went out running with Bess one day when the weather was dry and sunny and my mother didn't need my help in the house.

We came across a rabbit, which froze at our approach, but we had both seen it.

Although I was quite happy to eat rabbit, I have always been very soft hearted. I didn't want to see Bess kill a rabbit, particularly at close quarters. Bess crept towards the rabbit; she looked like a sheepdog circling sheep, nose well forward, body low, almost touching the ground. The rabbit didn't move.

I looked round for a stone to frighten the rabbit off. The only stone nearby was larger than I had intended using, but I threw it towards the rabbit, intending to miss it, which it did. The rabbit bolted just as Bess went for it; poor Bess got the stone on the head.

Staggering about, weak legged, with a lump like a pigeon egg on her head, Bess tried to get away from me. She couldn't understand why I had hit her on the head. Eventually I managed to drag her home, where she collapsed in a corner. "What happened to Bess?" my mother asked me, while she comforted Bess and examined the lump on her head.

I explained what had happened, expecting my soft hearted, but strict mother to be angry. Mother was very understanding. "You're just like me. I would have done the same thing, and probably would have hit poor Bess on the head too."

Bess recovered, but my brothers were disappointed at her reluctance to chase rabbits.

The artist Laird

White wood anemone

The Artist Laird

There have been Farquharsons at Finzean since 1579, but the best loved of all the Farquharson Lairds must have been Joseph Farquharson, the 12th laird of Finzean. He was a successful artist, who is probably best remembered for his paintings of sheep and snow. However, he is probably better remembered by many older people in the Finzean area as a kind and generous man, who knew everyone and spoke to everyone regardless of their position or financial situation.

The laird seemed to know my father well, although he was not one of the estate workers. When he saw me after I left school he remembered my name, and inquired how I had got on since leaving school.

The laird could be seen around Finzean at any time of the year. I can see him now, standing with a sketch pad in his hand, sitting at an easel, or just walking. He spoke pleasantly to everyone he met, but no one disturbed him while he was sketching or painting.

There were several mobile studios which he could use at any time of the year, as he preferred to paint the whole picture on the spot. He wasn't content doing a quick sketch on the spot, and painting the whole picture inside a studio. In this way he captured the light perfectly. If the weather changed, he would leave the canvas in the wooden, portable studio until the light conditions returned. Meanwhile he would start another painting elsewhere, or return to a previous one.

Some of his well known sheep paintings were slightly less authentic. He had three model sheep made by William Wilson of Monymusk, who cast the leopards of Union Bridge, Aberdeen. This helped him arrange the sheep in the landscape he painted, without worrying about the sheep wandering off. It also enabled him to paint the rest of the picture directly from nature. In later years his garden became one of his favourite subjects. Like the artist Claude Monet, he designed the garden himself making it spectacularly beautiful and full of rich colours. Among my personal memories of the laird are the Christmas parties, which we looked forward to for almost the whole year.

At the first Christmas party he gave me an exquisite, expensive doll. He also took time to speak to me and convinced me, to this day, that the doll chosen for me was very special, that it was the best of all the dolls given at that party. I wondered why I was fortunate enough to be chosen, picked out as someone special.

Each year the party grew bigger as the population increased, and boarded-out children were added to the school role. The parties were very up to date, with improvements made every year. To many children their only experience of Christmas was the Finzean parties. Lavish balls were also held in that same ballroom. At one time, members of the Royal Family attended, while they were at the "Balmoral Royal Estate". Many guests were invited to "Finzean House" during the hunting season. However, none of these fine guests could have appreciated the lairds generosity, as much as the children of "Finzean School".

One treasured memory I have of Joseph Farquharson came about when I was sent out with two other girls, by the teacher, to collect wild plants for nature study. We noticed the laird seated in front of an easel and should have left quietly to avoid disturbing him, but I wanted to get a closer look at his painting. I tried to get close enough to see his painting, but not disturb him. I got too close, but instead of complaining he called me over. My companions stayed back at first, as they were afraid we would get in trouble at school, but I was determined to see the painting, so I willingly went up to him.

Pleasantly he enquired, why we were not at school? When I told him about our hunt for wild flowers, he told us where to go for white wood anemones. Then he wanted to know if I painted, as I was so keen to see his painting. "No, but I think it would be wonderful to be able to paint pictures, but I'm not clever."

The laird laughed at this. "Anyone can learn to paint if they are interested enough and keep working at it, but it's best to start young." He then went on to describe how he would build up the picture, in layers, until the scene we were looking at would be recorded on canvas forever. By now my friends had joined us and were as interested as I was to hear what he was saying. Before we left he asked us our names, which really worried my companions. They thought he'd asked our names as he intended complaining about us to the school. They even persuaded me that we would be punished for getting too close.

Back at school I told the teacher that the laird had told us where to find the wood anemones, and had called us over. She repeated the warning that we must not disturb the laird when he was painting. She didn't tell us off, and he didn't complain to the school.

At the next Christmas party I received an artist's set of the best quality. There were enough pencils, sketch pads and paints to keep the children in our family busy for some time to come.

It has always been a dream of mine to own a Farquharson painting or print of the Finzean area. I had given up hope and was already going blind when John, my son, brought home a box of Christmas cards with two Farquharson snow scenes. I recognised the scenes right away and treasure these cards. If I hold them up very close to my eyes, and at the right angle, I can just make out the pictures. Recently I was given a larger Joseph Farquharson print, as "The Aberdeen Art Gallery" still sells his prints in their shop at an affordable price. I have been told that these prints are still very popular, after all these years.

My last memory of Joseph Farquharson is of Elsie, my youngest sister, coming home with tears in her eyes, to break the news that the laird was dead. Few lairds have ever been appreciated, loved or respected, as much as Joseph Farquharson.

Chrissie Gibson on a recent visit to Aberdeen Art Gallery in front of a Joseph Farquarson painting of Forest of Birse, a familiar childhood place.

A New Broom

*A*fter Miss Gill retired, we had a relief teacher for about six months. I don't think she would have stayed any longer if asked, as she was not at all suited to teaching in a small, country, primary school. This last relief teacher was a tall, young woman; who was over-qualified for primary school tuition. I believe she had a university degree and her ambition was to teach at an academy or grammar school.

Our new teacher was not used to country life; she had no experience of teaching a primary school, or of being in a mixed ability and mixed age groups class. She had no idea of how to deal with either infants or primary aged children. In other ways she was a competent teacher. We had learned little while we had a series of short term teachers. This teacher started making up lost ground. However, her main aim seemed to be to impose discipline on her class.

Discipline was imposed at every infringement of the school rules by use of the strap. Even the youngest children were given the full weight of our teacher as she brought the strap down on outstretched palms. Most of us were frightened of her, but the belt was being used so often that we could have become hardened by it. It seems ridiculous that the older children, in the headmaster's class, were usually only strapped for fighting or repeatedly being troublesome.

At that time my brother Jimmy, aged six years old, had recently started school. Jimmy was lucky to survive blood poisoning when he was a toddler. My parents were warned by the doctor that he would be a weak child for years to come, and that the illness might have caused permanent damage. We all looked after Jimmy and my parents never gave him a smack, as they did not know how weak he was.

When my mother heard how enthusiastic our teacher was on corporal punishment, Mother told me that I must not allow my brother Jimmy to get the strap. A letter had been sent to the headmaster when Jimmy started school, and a note was kept in the class register to remind teachers that they must not strap him. Mother knew that it was impossible, during severe weather conditions, to get to school on time every day. When we were going to school we all stayed together, so we could only travel at the speed of the slowest child. Jimmy tired easily and was more likely to trip or run into something, as he was blind in one eye. When the route was covered in snow and ice, it was even more difficult getting to school on time.

One morning we heard the bell being rung as we approached. The classes were already lined up when we ran through the school gate, so we were told to stand on one side and wait until the classes went in. Davie went into the headmaster's class unscathed, but our teacher had other ideas about us.

"You may think I am being hard on you all when you were only a minute late, but that is worse than being five minutes late. All you had to do to be on time was to leave home one minute earlier. Perhaps after the strap you'll all remember to leave home, one minute earlier in future."

She told us all to line up to receive the strap. I did as my mother instructed me to do, and reminded the teacher that Jimmy should not be strapped. The teacher insisted he would be strapped and told him to line up with the others. I begged her not to strap Jimmy, but that only made matters worse.

The teacher seemed to think I was trying to boss her about, or make a fool of her. "If you don't want your brother to get the strap, will you take his punishment for him?"

I didn't know what to say, so I just repeated what my mother had said about Jimmy not getting the strap. This made her very angry. "Either he takes his punishment, or you have to take it for him." I repeated my mother's message again, so she told me to hold out my hands.

I held my hands out in the usual manner, one on top of the other, and stared in terror as the strap was raised above the teacher's head. The swish as it was brought down, with the greatest force she could muster, stayed with me in nightmares for years afterwards. The pain from one smack was unbelievable, but she shouted at me again and again to replace my hands, forcing me to accept more pain. My palms were split and bleeding even before she came to my brother's share of the punishment.

"Are you still willing to accept your brother's punishment?" she demanded.

"Please don't strap my brother James, Miss. My mother says he is not able to take the strap." She just carried on, opening up the cuts and inflicting new cuts on my wrists and fingers, sending the pain to a new level. I would not cry for her, but I did think I was going to faint. For the rest of the day I was unable to hold anything, or to take part in any lessons. No attempt was made to bandage my bleeding hands, despite the cold weather waiting for me on the way home.

Davie put my gloves onto my hands for me, as he was worried about my hands becoming frostbitten. I ran home in a state of shock, holding my hands out in front of me as if I was trying to hold the pain away. As the blood turned to ice the pain got even worse for a while. On the last mile or so I couldn't feel anything at all. Davie ran ahead, on the last few yards, to tell Mother.

Mother was shocked by the appearance of my hands. The gloves were soaked with blood which had turned to ice. Quickly she poured warm water in a basin, and added salt. Then as I soaked my hands in the warm water, she cut the gloves off. Lumps of ice were sticking in the cuts. She was afraid to remove these right away as the sharp edges could have added to the damage.

The feeling started returning to my hands, in the form of pain. Now I was home I could keep my feelings back no longer,

I was screaming in agony. Someone was sent to the nearest phone, to phone for the doctor. This was almost unheard of in those days. My hands were held in warm salted water until the doctor arrived. By now their colour had improved, and gangrene looked less likely.

The doctor wrote a letter to the education authorities, stating the condition of my hands. This was included with my mother's letter of complaint. Mother complained that it was unfair to give a child punishment due to another child.

A man came to investigate the complaint, and also to look at my hands. He said that the problem could not be dealt with by our local education authority, as we crossed the county border when we went to school. He also said that under the circumstances, I had volunteered to take the strap. "Don't volunteer to take the strap for any reason in the future. Your teacher would not have given the strap to your brother because of the note she had." I pointed out that she had him in line to be strapped with the others.

I was also asked what I thought of the teacher. I told him she was the only teacher to teach us anything since Miss Gill left. That I would prefer not to change to another teacher, who might not teach us anything at all. "Well said," was his reply.

A report was sent to the other education authority. Our teacher was told to walk the same route herself, that we normally took to school, and then judge whether or not we should have been punished for being one minute late for school. After walking from the school to our house, the teacher came to our door and apologised to Mother.

"I'm very sorry. I had no idea of the distance, or the rough ground your children have to cover on their way to school." She was more understanding when children who had to walk a long distance to school were late, after her own long trek, and she used the belt less often to punish minor offences.

My fingers were stiff and awkward, and I lacked feeling in my hands for a long time after the strapping incident. When I returned to school, the headmaster asked to see my hands. He had known nothing about the incident until the education authorities informed him. "I'm sorry Christina, I didn't know your hands were as bad as that." He was very sympathetic and assured me that I would not get the strap for being late for school, in future.

I can't remember ever being strapped at school again.

I got on better with the teacher after that. She realised I was keen to learn and found time to give me a bit of extra tuition. Sometimes she asked me to stay behind for a short time after class, and help her tidy up. Then she would say. "You'd better go now Christina, I'd better not keep you too late as I know you've a long way to go."

Just before her six months were up she asked me to stay behind and help her clear out some of her own books from the cupboard, and carry them down to her digs. She called at the mobile shop on the way, and I waited outside. When we parted, at her digs, she gave me a large, red apple as a reward for being so helpful. I felt it was also her way of saying sorry.

I proudly took the apple home. It was the biggest apple I had ever seen. My mother sliced it into portions so I could share my reward with my brothers and sisters. When Mother saw the inside was pink, she said. "You are lucky. This is an American Jonathan apple. It's my favourite apple, but I don't usually buy them as they're expensive." Jonathan apples became my favourite type of apple too. After I left school, and had some money of my own, I sometimes bought a couple of pounds of Jonathan apples to take home to my brothers and sisters.

When I look back on these events I would like to say that the apple was a satisfactory conclusion to an unhappy event, but I can't. Although I believe in soldiering on despite setbacks, and making the best I can of any situation, the situation should never have arisen. In this case the damage was already done. Getting another inexperienced teacher would not have helped me. I can't forget the ordeal I was put through, even after sixty seven years.

I have permanent scars on both my palms, in the form of hard ridges under the top layer of skin. Every day since the wounds healed, I have had to exercise my hands before grasping anything, or I am likely to drop whatever I pick up. This could be pretty dangerous when picking up a hot pot or kettle, particularly when there are small children about. For a time it was thought I would never have full use of my hands. There is also the pain and mental anguish I was subjected to.

Teachers seemed to be immune from prosecution in those days for anything short of murder. My memory of the event still sends a cold shiver through me. I was only ten years old and tiny for my age, so the teacher, who was taller than my father, seemed almost like a giant to me as she brought the belt down from a great height.

I can't think of this event for long. I have to push it to the back of my other memories, before I start taking nightmares again, reliving this event after nearly seventy years. No amount of apples could soothe the nightmares I suffered, for years after the ordeal.

The Harmonium

I don't remember how many weeks I was off school as a result
of the damage inflicted by the belt, but the state my hands
were in after the surface cuts healed was harder to come to
terms with than the pain inflicted at the time. The healing process
was more traumatic than receiving the belt, as being in a state of
shock helps by numbing the mind. Being completely dependant
on others, unable to even dress or undress without help and
having to be fed like a toddler at the age of ten years is very
depressing. I just wanted things to be back to normal, and
imagined that when the bandages were removed that I would be
completely recovered. I was wrong.

When the deep cuts in my palms, fingers and wrists healed,
my hands were rigid and the fingers healed straight, like steel
pokers. Unable to bend the fingers on either hand, I couldn't
even massage my own hands to try and release the solid joints.
Mother, Father and other members of the family massaged my
hands to no avail. The doctor said I would never have full use

of my hands. I was determined to prove him wrong.

My first attempts to get the joints moving was very painful. I put the back of my hand on the table and leaned my weight on it, while pulling my palm and wrist back towards myself, with all the force I could muster. The pain was terrible, but my fingers bent stiffly making my hands look like talons. I forced my fingers in both hands back and fore in this manner until I regained slight movements in my fingers. I carried on with this painful, forced movements, until I could hold a pencil for a minute or two. When I returned to school my hands were kept in my pockets while I was outside and I tried to hide them when I was in the classroom, as I was embarrassed by their claw-like appearance.

In class at times, the frustration of trying to write reduced me to tears of anger as I wrenched my fingers about, and banged them on the desk, trying to force them into the positions they needed to be in. I expected to be like this for the rest of my life, but I kept on abusing my hands, as if I was punishing them for being useless.

At home I picked up the chanter that I had been learning to play and tried to play a scale – it was hopeless! My father watched me and said nothing, but I'm sure he had an idea of how I could be helped. He found a less painful way of improving the flexibility of my hands and I didn't even realise what I was doing.

A few days later I returned home from school to the beautiful mellow tones of an organ, which seemed to be coming from our house. I ran into the house and tracked down the sound to my brothers' bedroom, which was the only area in the house with enough space to take a fairly large organ. Mother was playing this beautiful instrument, of polished wood, which had "Harmonium" in raised letters across the front. I watched Mother work the foot-pedals and use the organ stops to vary the tone. She was playing quite a simple tune, but after a few minutes she started making mistakes, which she couldn't seem to get right. She must have been rusty, as she hadn't played an organ for a while. She left the organ to make us a cup of tea and a snack, which we always had when we came home from school. She told us that Father bought the organ at a roup at Aboyne. During the next couple of days I watched Mother trying to get to grips with the organ and not quite managing it.

I would watch her play a pleasant tune, perhaps an easy bagpipe tune, like the ones I was playing on the chanter before my hands were damaged. Just as I was really enjoying the music she would make a silly mistake, which she would struggle to put right. Then she would have to go off and do something before she had the hang of the tune. The organ was a great temptation to me, which I struggled to resist, as I didn't think I could play it, the way my hands were. In the end I gave in to temptation and tried the notes on the keyboard, out of curiosity. To my surprise, unlike the piano, they required hardly any pressure from my hands. I tried a simple scale and found to my surprise that it was not too difficult. Now I could attempt a simple pipe tune, which required a lot of practice and patience. As I learned this simple tune, my hands were beginning to loosen, to become more useful. I was also being rewarded for my efforts with the satisfaction of learning music, by ear, on an instrument I adored.

I stopped worrying about my hands never being as useful as they used to be.

My brothers' complained about me always being in their bedroom, but my father told then to leave me alone. This encouraged me to carry on practising, as my father's approval meant a lot to me. The more tunes I learned, the more ambitious I became. When father bought a wireless, when I was older, I learned to play the semi classical music, which was popular on the wireless at the time. No one told me that the organ was brought into the house as a sort of exercise therapy for my injured hands, but that is how it turned out. I felt that I had made the instrument my own and was proud of my achievement. I was never invited to play the organ, or offered lessons, which would have been beyond the use of my poor hands at the time. It was just there to tempt me, and my parents made sure it was available for me when I wanted to play it.

I know now that I owe the remarkable recovery of my hands to that vacant harmonium seat, which was a temptation to me. No one suggested I even try to play it, no one said I shouldn't, so there was no pressure on me at all. I know now how wise my parents were, but if I had realised what they were thinking at the time, I wonder if my wonderful organ would have been so attractive.

Schoolchildren, c. 1920

School Friendship

*A*fter the first two or three years, when I was frequently punched, kicked and had my hair pulled, I made friends with a number of children, including younger children. Younger children became attached to our group as they knew we wouldn't bully them, or allow anyone else to pick on younger children. However, I was only a child myself and couldn't foresee all dangers, which nearly ended in tragedy for Wee Jimmy.

The Runaway Sledge

In winter sledging was a popular pastime among Finzean Bairns, as even when there is no snow falling, snow and ice can lie for a week or more in fields and other placed where it doesn't have to be cleared. Sledges were often brought part of the way to school and left in favourite sledging places. After school, these slopes were busy with sledging children as long as there was enough light to see where they were going. Normally I didn't take part as we couldn't get our sledges over the stiles. I didn't borrow anyone else's sledge as the most popular sledging field belonged to Sniffy's father, who always seemed to be complaining about something. On the one occasion that I did take part, it put me off sledging for life.

I stopped to watch some of my friends sledging on my way home from school. "Wee Jimmy", who was only five years old at the time, asked me to sit on the back of his sledge as there were no smaller children about. "Go on Chris, I've been waiting aboot here for ages. There's naebody else, and the sledge is too big for me on my ain."

I refused at first as I was nine or ten years old at the time and I felt that my weight was too much for him to control. His sledge was controlled by a movable section at the front, which was guided by pulling a rope attached to the left or right side. "I dinna think it's a good idea, Jimmy. If you canna turn the sledge it will go too fast and crash at the bottom o' the brae."

Jimmy was very persuasive. "I've done it afore, Chris. Even wae bigger bairns on the back. Look I can turn the ski's at the front."

I tried pushing Jimmy on a gentle slope. He could control the sledge as long as I pushed it, but it came to a stop within a short distance. He really did need extra weight, but I was still reluctant to sit on the back even for one run, so Jimmy argued on.

"I dinna think this is a good idea, Jimmy. The brae looks too steep to me. You have tae be able tae turn before the steepest bit, or you'll go oot o' control."

"I've done it afore, I can control the sledge, sit on the back, Chris. It'll be alright." He was so keen to go and I didn't want to disappoint him that I let him talk me into it. We got on the sledge and as we pushed off I reminded him, "Remember to turn to the left Jimmy!"

We set off at a much quicker pace than I had expected. After several days of sledging, the slope was pure, smooth ice and very soon we were out of control. "Turn the sledge now Jimmy, turn to the left."

"It winna turn Chris, I've already pulled tae the left." I knew my weight was making the problem worse.

"I'll get aff, Jimmy, then try again." I dug my feet into the ground. My bottom hit the cold ice with a painful thump and I carried on sliding down the hill, while the sledge went straight on still gaining speed. Just as I came to a stop the sledge crashed at the foot of the hill and I saw Wee Jimmy being thrown into the air. I knew he would land in a deep water filled ditch and might drown, if the fall didn't kill him. As I ran screaming down the hill, all the other children abandoned their sledges and followed me. I couldn't see Jimmy at first as I ran towards the ditch, then he surfaced among lumps of ice. He floated for long enough for me to get hold of him until the others arrived. His clothes were now waterlogged and the extra weight was pulling him down. Screaming, "Are you alright, Jimmy? Are you alright?" I managed to pull him to the edge of the ditch, where other hands helped to pull him out. His eyes were open, but I still thought he was dead.

"Aye, I'm alright. It's nae you're fault Chrissie, you did warn me." White faced and shivering, he was still trying to assure me that it wasn't my fault. I suppose that's one of the reasons we all liked Jimmy so much.

"Go straight hame, Jimmy. Tell your mother you've been in the ditch. Dinna try and hide it, you'll have tae get dried properly and get intae some dry clothes." Jimmy didn't have far to go, but I couldn't hang about as I was quite wet myself and I had three miles still to go, but I walked part of the way with him.

"Remember to tell your Ma what happened, Jimmy. I'm sorry if you get in trouble o'wer this. Will your Ma punish you for ruining you school clothes, Jimmy?"

"Ma will be too relieved to see that I'm alright tae punish me." Jimmy was obviously speaking from past experiences. Jimmy was unharmed by his accident and never blamed me.

For weeks after the accident I expected Jimmy's father to complain to my father, as I thought I was old enough to know better. I felt responsible and also guilty, but no accusation came. When I saw Jimmy fly through the air and heard him plunge into the icy water, I thought I had killed him. Even if he survived the crash I knew he could drown in the icy water; that we might not be able to get him up from the bottom in time. Then I worried for days about him catching pneumonia, or that he might have other injuries that we hadn't noticed at the time. Next day at school he acted as if nothing had happened, I don't think he even caught a cold from his experience.

Although I avoided the crash and felt guilty about getting off the sledge, if I had stayed on the sledge my weight landing on top of him might have killed Jimmy. The crash still put me off sledging for good as even a gentle slope, with no dangers at the foot, made me nervous. As for the sledging field, children are probably still sledging down it every winter.

Groups of friends.

As most families were large in the twenties and thirties, we tended to make friends in groups. When Sandy became a special friend, his two cousins were also friendly with my family group. We also tended to be more friendly with children who lived on our route to school. When I was older, Frank, who sat next to me at school, and his sister Elsie became close friends. Elsie was older than me, but she seemed more sensible, and kind hearted then most of the girls of my age. When I was eleven years old I took on the responsibility of carrying milk home from their father's dairy, which was about half a mile from the school, on our way home.

I carried a five pint flagon with me in the mornings, and left it at the dairy. Elsie had the task of delivering three or four flagons of milk on her way to school, and of picking up the empty flagons on the way back. Elsie was given a snack, usually a scone, at each of these houses, which she shared with me. If she got an apple she would split it neatly in two, by gripping the apple in her hands and pulling the sides apart. When I picked up the full flagon of milk on the way back, Elsie's mother always gave me a scone, or a cake, or a piece of fruit. Near Christmas, she gave me a tangerine and if I had one of my younger brothers or sisters with me, they were given one too.

The whole family were pleasant and kind hearted. Their mother must have been an excellent cook, as the scones and cakes were delicious. When Frank and Elsie's father bought a car, he used it as a taxi. It was the only one in our area. Elsie was keen to learn to drive just as soon as she was old enough. I used to see her sometimes, driving her father's taxi, which encouraged me to learn to drive too. I passed my driving test, at the age of seventeen years, in a Model T Ford, which were common at the time. While we were both at school, we were content to be close friends. Another family we were friendly with, lived much nearer our home.

Muggie was also slightly older than me. She called me her best friend, and used to come over to our house sometimes. She had an older brother, Alick, who was fascinated by my hair. At that time my hair was still blonde. In my teens my hair turned brown, but at that time Alick said my hair shone more than any of the other lassie's hair, in the school. He had a comical rhyme which he used to repeat if he saw me.

Sand Martins will hear you farting
when flying through the air.
If you're nae a bonnie lassie,
They'll take you by the hair.

He would then make a grab for my hair, which made me indignant. "Don't you dare pull my hair Alick." That would make us both laugh, as he never pulled my hair. He was one of the few boy's at school that didn't pull my hair at some time during my schooling.

Muggie and Alick's mother was a nice woman. I used to buy eggs from their farm when our hens didn't lay enough for our own use. I would go to their farm on the way home from school, sometimes. We also bought their own make of butter from them and also vegetables. Muggie would let me know when they opened a pit of tatties in the winter. I always asked her mother to keep two bags of one hundredweight of tatties for us, which were picked up at the weekend. They had Kerr's pinks tatties which were my mothers favourite type of tattie. The tatties were stored in large, earthen pits over winter, which protected them from the frost. If there was a spell of frost, the pits couldn't be opened until the frosty spell was over. Only enough potatoes were taken out each time, to last for a few weeks. If there was a long frosty spell and you ran out of potatoes, then you just had to do without for a while. Mother always bought enough tatties to make sure we always had at least half a bag left, next time she expected the pits to be opened. Most of our food was bought straight from the local farms, but it was also wise to have a few tins of milk and other non-perishable foods, in case we had a spell of bad weather.

These were just a few of my friends during my school years, but these are the ones I remember best.

Daydreaming

The standard of education in an overcrowded two roomed school was bound to be lower than the average city school, and boringly repetitive after the first three years. I began to feel as if I had heard every lesson over and over again, and knew every next word. Sitting at the back of the class makes concentration more difficult, and I sometimes felt as if the teacher didn't even know I was there.

Daydreaming was far more interesting. I would think about my journey to school that morning and wonder how far the birds were progressing with nest building. I would also wonder about the underground burn, where it really came from? Would we ever find it? My mind was a free spirit wandering the hills and visiting places which were too far from our normal route to school for us to reach.

A painful rap on the head suddenly wrenched me from my daydream. Our teacher was standing beside me, with the blackboard pointer in her hand, demanding to know what she had just said. She must have hit me harder than she intended as I now had a very painful headache. Holding my hand on the painful spot and with tears in my eyes I complained.

"That was very painful Miss. You're not supposed to hit us with a pointer."

The question was repeated. When I couldn't tell her what she said, she asked "What is so interesting outside Christina, that you are not paying attention to your lessons?"

I didn't want to admit that I had been daydreaming. I looked out of the window in search of an excuse. In the far distance I spotted a tiny dot which I guessed was an aeroplane. I could just hear the faint drone of its engine. "Look Miss. Look at that aeroplane in the distance." The teacher couldn't see anything at first; she must have thought that I had wonderful eyesight. "Listen to its engine, I think there's something wrong with it."

We both stared out of the window at the dot, which was now beginning to take shape. My instinct about the plane's engine was right. The engine started to falter, the plane started to lose height and then went into a dive. The engine started to fire again and the plane climbed. "I think you're right Christina. The aeroplane does seem to be in trouble."

There was a sudden loud rumble as the whole class rushed to the windows to see the aeroplane. It was a biplane, possibly an old plane from the "Great War." As it came nearer the engine faltered again and it went into another dive, then recovered. This happened again, but by now the plane was quite near the school. As it approached the school it was flying pretty low, when the engine faltered again. The whole class seemed to be hypnotised by the approaching biplane, which looked as if it was coming down.

"Oh my God, it's heading for the school", I called out in panic when I realised that the plane was so close that I could see the pilot. We all ducked down, as if that could save any of us in a plane crash. The engine roared and the plane climbed, just short of the school, threatening to loosen slates and remove the weather vane from the roof.

The whole school shook as the biplane passed over. We could hardly believe that it cleared the school. The headmaster rushed into our classroom; as the plane made so much noise going over, he thought the school had been hit. He inspected the school from the outside, then he came back and assured us that no damage had been done. He was by now very angry as there was no warning from his side of the school, just the sound of the engine seconds before the near miss.

"I think I'll complain to the authorities", he told our teacher. I put up my hand. "Sir, please Sir, the aeroplane seemed to be in trouble. It sounded like a car we had for a short while. The engine was always misfiring so it couldn't climb the hills. My father had to get rid of it and go back to using a horse."

The headmaster had a car of his own and knew what I meant. The teacher described the plane's erratic flight, so the headmaster decided to give the pilot the benefit of the doubt. We resumed our lessons, and there was no further mention of me staring out of the window or daydreaming.

The Ghostly Figure
on the Moor

*I*t must have been a week or two after my twelfth birthday and about a week before our Christmas holidays, when I was foolish enough to walk home on my own in near darkness. It was toffee making time at school as we neared the Christmas concert. The younger children were let out early, so our teacher could supervise the older girls while we made the toffee.

On previous toffee making evenings I walked home with Muggie. Neither of us seem to think that the way home might be dangerous in darkness. Muggie was off school ill and without her help I was probably even later than usual leaving the school. It was probably about a quarter past four when I finally left school and headed for the dairy for my full, five pint flagon of milk. By the time I opened the gate to the moor I could only see vague outlines. I was beginning to realise how silly I was to leave school so late on my own. If I fell in the darkness on the moor and injured myself, who would hear me? It would be more than an hour before anyone realised I was late, and Mother thought I was with Muggie. I was closing the gate when I was startled by a sound, almost like a moan.

"What was that noise?" I wondered for a few seconds, straining to hear more clearly. There it was again. I held my breath for a few seconds. "Sheep! It was the sound that sheep made when they were unhappy about something." I listened for a minute or two until I realised the sound came from the direction of a hollow across the moor, which sheep and cattle sometimes had difficulty getting out of if they weren't used to the moor. They weren't in any real danger, but I was surprised to hear them as there had been no sheep on the moor for a while. There were none on the moor when I went to school that morning. I set off running along the rough farm track; trying to get as near as possible to home before complete darkness hid even these vague outlines. The flagon always made a loud clink, clank sound as I ran, which I found annoying when I was on my own. I hadn't gone far when the outline of an unusually tall man became obvious in the distance. I ran on expecting him to call out in a reassuring way, letting me know that he was a neighbour. On previous occasions, when we approached a farmer or farm worker, he would call out our names or "Hurry up lassies, your mother will be wonderin' whit's happened tae you." On this occasion the man was silent and still, which made me feel uneasy. I slowed down as I realised the man must be a stranger. He was taller than all the local men and also thinner. I began wondering if he was a ghost as he was so quiet, completely still and wore an unusual bonnet; not the usual flat cap that the farm workers wore. I almost turned and ran in panic. Then I realised he was wearing a coachman's tippet and my feeling of panic turned to real fear, as I thought of another reason for the stranger's presence.

At this time there was still stories of body snatchers circulating. These stories were usually told in whispers, with knowing looks that suggested the medical schools still bought fresh bodies, without asking any questions about the cause of death. My pace slowed even more as I thought of the possibility of a cart or coach waiting nearby to whisk my dead body away. Thick bushes and trees on one side of the track and a steep slope on the other side left me little room to pass the stranger. If I turned back it wouldn't take a man long to catch up with me so heart racing I decided to face him and hit him with the flagon if I was attacked. As I drew closer I realised there were two dogs beside him and the stranger spoke.

"Have you seen any lost sheep on the moor Lassie? Four o' my sheep are missing. I've just been quietly listening for them, and told the dogs to be quiet, but I canna hear them."

Obviously the stranger was a shepherd who had rented winter grazing from one of the local farmers. By the direction he came from, his flock must have been grazing on Muggie's father's farm. I told him where to find the sheep I had heard earlier. He seemed quite concerned at the state I was in.

"Thanks Lassie, now hurry hame, there's naebody else hanging aboot on the wye hame, and be careful crossing that stile in the dark."

"I'm used to that stile. I could cross it blindfolded, but you gave me a right scare standin' quietly. I thought you were hidin'. You took a year aff my life wae the rate my heart is poundin'. I was ready to hit you on the head wae my milk flagon."

"You got a scare! You were makin' so much noise wae that flagon, wae the clink, clank noise it makes, just like horse harness coming towards me, but no horse. I coulna' see you at first because you're so little. How do you think I felt? I thought you were a ghost."

The shepherd went off in the direction I pointed out to him and I ran home vowing I would never make that journey alone again in the dark. When I told my mother about the stranger on the moor, I thought she was going to take a heart attack. "Don't you dare do that again. If the teacher wants toffee made then she can finish the job herself."

Next day Muggie was back at school. By the time I had finished telling her about the ghostly figure on the moor, she was probably nervous about crossing it in daylight, with an escort. Even together we made sure we got away before darkness, when we stayed late to make toffee.

Scarlet Fever

The Summer break of 1932 was very enjoyable as it was a long, hot, dry summer. It was late August, almost time for the schools to go back, when I caught scarlet fever.

Father took us to be measured for our new school clothes. Although I was twelve years old I was still small for my age and assumed that I would always be small and slim, like my sister Mary. My new kilt was still the style with its own bodice, like the younger children wore, and the tailoress said I had hardly grown in the last year so, my new kilt was only an inch longer than the old one.

A day or two later Mary came home for a few days, as she was between employers. Mary was in service at the time and had managed to find employment nearer home, so she could come home more often and didn't have to travel so far on her day off.

Mary awoke next morning with a painful, swollen throat. She thought it was an infection caused by a fly she'd almost swallowed, several days before. As she had no rash the doctor thought she was right and only had tonsillitis, with an abscess on one of her tonsils. The usual treatment was to gargle salt and water, which made Mary vomit.

Unfortunately, I cleaned up the mess and also caught scarlet fever. My brother Geordie was two and a half years old at the time. He was very attached to me and used to follow me about, so he picked up the germ from me. By the time I started to feel ill and the rash appeared, Mary was very ill. My father phoned the doctor and told him about the rash and Geordie's inflamed throat, so the doctor came straight away.

The fever hospital in Aboyne was full, due to the effect of the lengthy spell of hot weather, so we were sent to the fever hospital at Inverurie by ambulance. Cars and vans were becoming more common and the old horse drawn ambulances had been replaced by a motor powered van. It was really just an ordinary van. There was no special equipment in case of emergencies and the driver was just a driver, with no first aid training.

When we were admitted to hospital we had to change into hospital nightwear. No one was allowed to wear their own nightie or pyjamas. The clothes we were wearing were only returned after they were washed by the hospital. The main role of the fever hospitals was to isolate people with serious, infectious illnesses to cut down the spread of disease.

While we were there the nurses were very kind to us, but we were split up. Mary's illness was more advanced than mine, so she went to a different ward. As Geordie was only a toddler he was put in a ward for younger children who needed more attention, so that the nurses could look after him better. By the time I arrived at the fever hospital I was getting steadily worse. I could hear Geordie crying and calling for me continuously. This made my illness worse. I was hardly able to lift my head, but I knew Geordie was refusing to eat or sleep, which could make an already serious illness fatal.

My father cycled to Inverurie on the next Sunday, which was the only visiting day. We could only see one another through a closed window, but I knew he was asking me why Geordie was in a different ward. Father told me to ask the nurses to bring Geordie through to my ward to calm him down. Eventually, they relented and brought his cot through to the foot of my bed. He was supposed to stay in his cot, but he climbed out and crawled up my bed, into my arms, where he fell asleep. The nurse was able to put him, still sleeping, back into his own cot.

The only treatment for scarlet fever then was good nursing, such as tepid sponging when our fever was high, and painting our tonsils and throat with a tar like substance, which had an unpleasant, bitter taste. The tarry substance was painted on with a swab which looked to me as if it was a piece of a white blanket. It was probably thick white lint, but it felt as if the nurse was trying to push a whole blanket down my throat.

After my throat was painted, which happened twice a day, it was Geordie's turn. I got him to open his mouth for the nurse by telling him that if he didn't do exactly what the nurses told him to do, he would be put back into the other ward. Then I held his head still, while the nurse swabbed his throat.

Geordie became very ill and for a while I thought he was going to die in my arms. He was very lucky to recover from scarlet fever and to have no lasting damage to his health.

Mother didn't visit for several weeks as she thought her presence would make Geordie worse. I told him that he would be allowed to see Mother through the window, but only if he didn't cry for her. Then I repeated the warning that if he got upset, he would go back to the other ward. He was good for me during the remainder of our stay.

There was another boy of the same name and age who came from Glasgow. He had no visitors as his parents were in Aberdeen on holiday when Georgie became ill. His mother had to go back to Glasgow without him. He cried himself to sleep every night, repeating the same words over and over again. "Georgie's Mammie come back for Georgie." The nurses were very kind to him and repeatedly assured him that his Mammie would be coming back soon to take him home.

One of the most upsetting experiences for me was seeing a bunch of my hair on the pillow. I lost quite a lot of hair and the nurses tried to comfort me by telling me my hair would grow back in again in no time. They wouldn't bring me a mirror until I knew I would be getting home in a few days; perhaps it was a wise decision. I was proud of my hair. My thick, blonde shining hair was truly my crowning glory, and I knew it wouldn't be anything to be proud of for some time. The remaining hair when I did see it was damaged and dead looking, after spending so much time on complete bed rest. I was also very homesick, but I knew I was in for several months and I just had to put up with it.

For a few days I seemed to be getting better, and was allowed to sit on the edge of the bed, then I was allowed to take a few steps. Unfortunately, I became ill again as my kidneys gave me problems for a few days. When my kidneys recovered, I knew I would soon be getting home but I was still very weak.

Recovering from Scarlet Fever

When I was admitted to the fever hospital I was given a small bed, more suitable for a seven year old. The bed was big enough for me when I arrived, but after two or three weeks my feet were sticking out of the end of the bed. We were gradually moved from ward to ward, as our condition improved, so when I moved on to another ward they just gave me a bigger bed.

I began to realize how much I had grown; when I was allowed to walk about the ward as everything seemed lower. I seemed to be much taller than the toddlers but I still felt as if I were a child. I also began to take an interest in my surroundings. I had never lived in a house with gas lighting, so the gas lights in the hospital interested me. A maintenance man came round one day to clean the gas light fittings. The gas flame provided light by spreading out over a gas mantle. The old gas mantles were very fragile, even when new, but I imagine they would also have been quite expensive. The man very gently removed the mantles without breaking one. He very gently put the tray of mantles down on a table, and left the ward. I had a closer look at these curious objects, which I imagined were used up and about to be replaced. I poked one of them, and it just crumbled to dust. This seemed like fun so I poked the remaining dozen or so mantles too. When the man came back a few minutes later, there was just a pile of dust on the tray.

The maintenance man was so angry, and shouted at me so loudly, that I hid under the bed. The ward sister came in to see what the commotion was about. She told him quite firmly that the mantles were his own responsibility and he should be more careful in future. "They shouldn't be left lying around."

When the time came for me to dress in my own clothes, and walk around the grounds, I couldn't get into my kilt and jumper. I was so disappointed that I wouldn't be able to wear my new kilt that I cried. One of the nurses told me that I would need much bigger clothes in future. "Don't worry, I'll get you a warm dressing gown and slippers to walk around outside in." I was now so tall even Geordie noticed and started asking me why I was now so big. Although I was allowed to help look after my brother Geordie while I was in hospital, I didn't get to see my sister Mary until it was almost time to go home. At that time the fever hospitals rotated their patients from cases in the early stages of scarlet fever in the admission ward to other wards dealing with the different stages of the illness. Patients gradually worked their way through the hospital to a discharge ward. As Mary's illness was at a later stage, due to late diagnosis, she started off two or three wards ahead of us. The wards were also isolated from one another. When Mary was ready to go home, we were also discharged to be cared for at home. First we had to get used to the cooler air outside for a few days before we could go home.

It was good to get outside after eight weeks in bed, but I felt funny. I didn't seem to have control of my limbs any more. I couldn't hold a pencil properly, so one of the nurses wrote to my parents giving them my measurements. The letter had to be written in pencil and snipped at the corners so it could be steam treated to try and avoid passing on infection from the hospital.

When it was time to go home my father handed in our clothes the previous day, and he stayed overnight with relatives. We were taken to a discharge area, where we changed out of hospital clothes and had a bath. We then changed into the clothes which were handed in the previous day.

We left hospital in style, as my father's cousin took us home in his car. It was a large, comfortable, warm car, with a cloth roof. That was the most common type of car roof at the time. Mary was able to walk to the car unaided, but Father told me to stay by the door while he carried Geordie to the car. I felt I would be able to walk to the car, so I tried to follow him. My legs were like jelly. I was unable to control them, and had no sense of balance, so I tottered into a roughcast wall which gave me a headache and a bruised face.

My mother was very happy to see us home. She looked at me in my married, oldest sister's dress which was too short now that I was almost as tall as my father, and she knew how I felt.

She hugged me and said "My we lassie went intae hospital a bairn, and in two months she's come back a woman."

I felt cheated out of a large part of my childhood. There was no gradual change and no warning. My body had rushed through all the stages of puberty within a very short time. I felt not only weak and unhappy, but for a time I was very clumsy. I had missed about half of the school year before I was well enough to go back. I had also missed out on my year in the headmaster's class, as someone else was given my place. I missed the school concert and the Christmas party. Some of my older friends left school, so I missed their last few weeks. Others of my age were in the headmaster's class, and I wasn't exactly happy to return to a class where I now dwarfed all of the other children. I didn't look forward at all to going back to school.

Leap-Frog

When I was at last allowed to return to school it was only for a short while. The last teacher I had at school was, unlike the series of temporary teachers, a very enthusiastic teacher. She stayed at Finzean School until she married, several years after I left.

This teacher was a cheerful, lively young woman who had as colourful a personality, as her bright red hair. Her thick, red, bouncy, hair was very striking. She was likely to go into a fit of the giggles, seeing the funny aspect of something other teachers were likely to punish with one or two strokes of the strap on each hand. The children, especially the younger ones, absolutely adored her but I just felt out of place.

I had lost my place in the headmaster's class due to scarlet fever. I was also now about half way through the school year, so if someone did leave I would be unlikely to be able to catch up. Next school year, as my birthday was on December 6th, I would only have a few weeks in the headmaster's class before I had to leave on my fourteenth birthday.

There was nothing more I could learn in the teacher's class, so I spent my time helping the first and second years with their lessons. Although I enjoyed helping the teacher, I was very disappointed that I had missed the chance to improve my standard of reading, writing and general knowledge. I was still coming to terms with my vigorous growing spurt. I still felt inside as if I was a little girl, but I tired easily, and I tended to take cramp which was very painful. If I didn't stretch the muscle immediately, it went into an involuntary spasm.

My mother felt that I was wasting my time and had gone back to school too early; she wrote to the school authorities requesting my exemption from the remainder of my schooling. She told them that she needed me at home. She was now about fifty, but my youngest brother, Robert, was only two years old. He was her fifteenth baby.

While I waited for the exemption certificate to come through, I carried on helping the teacher. Our teacher was keen on physical education. Unfortunately there was no games park, gymnasium or equipment, so she tried to improvise. One day she announced that she was going to teach us a new exercise called leap-frog.

I was the only one tall enough to assist her with a demonstration on how it should be done. This worried me as I felt there was not really enough room in our class to play leap-frog safely. After several demonstration leaps, I warned the teacher that I was tired and needed to straighten up. Cheerfully, as she was enjoying herself, she said "Just one more jump. Watch carefully children!"

However, I had been bending over too long. A sudden pain in my neck was followed by a spasm, which jerked my head up just as she was going over. My head caught in her skirt and she landed on her head on the wooden classroom floor. I tried to help her up but I couldn't bend over any farther, I was forced to straighten up. My apologies were drowned out by the laughter of the whole class at the sight of our teacher.

Our teacher was sitting on the floor, red faced. Her clothes were dishevelled, and her untidy, red hair made her look like a dazed gonk. I just had to join in the laughter, expecting to get told off; but she apologised to me instead. "It was my own fault Christina. Are you alright? Is your neck or back strained?"

I was glad the P.E. lesson finished quickly, as I was afraid one of the children would have a crash landing on one of the desks. I hope that was the last time she tried to teach leap-frog in a classroom.

The muscular spasms proved to be quite a problem, in a classroom full to bursting point with small children. On my last day at school, I had to sit at one of the smallest desks to be near several children that I was helping. I took cramp and couldn't get out of the desk in time. I called for the teacher to help me out but she took one of her fits of the giggles. As usual the class joined in and despite being in pain I joined in too. The result was a powerful muscular spasm which forced my knees through the desk. I had quite a problem getting free from the tiny, old-fashioned desk, which had a fixed seat. This was accompanied by even more laughter, but I was lucky not to suffer permanent injury.

Although my exemption from school had not come through, the headmaster decided that there was no point in me staying any longer. He gave me a letter saying an official exemption letter would follow in a few days. I didn't even have to wait until the end of the school day. My two younger brothers, younger sister and my niece, were disappointed by the sudden end to my school days, but I felt as if I'd had enough of Finzean School, and was looking forward to helping mother with my youngest sister and two youngest brothers.

My last return journey was taken alone, and was full of regret. It was the part of my schooling that I was going to miss most. The birds were building their nests, and I realized that I wouldn't see their chicks, or see their first flights this year. I stopped at the quarry pool, and remembered all the fun we'd had there. I used to wonder, in winter, where all the toads and frogs disappeared to. Did they sleep at the bottom of the deepest part of the pond, or go away like migrating birds?

As I walked slowly back home, I decided that I would take an occasional walk to school with my brothers, sisters and nieces. I always took them to school for the first time, until I left home for good. Now that I'm old, blind and lame, I spend many hours thinking back on my childhood and comparing it to the life children have today.

We had a hard life, but a healthy lifestyle. We were well cared for. My mother was always there when we got home and she was always interested in our day. She was interested to hear about our lessons, about what went on and who did what? She was always ready to answer questions, if possible. She was very knowledgeable about nature. She always knew the names of the wild flowers, which we brought home. We never told Mother about the frogs, as she would have worried and ordered us to stay away from the pool. I can't even imagine coming home to an empty house as a child; or of coming home to an uncaring or uninterested household.

Too many children of today get in trouble because their mothers go out to work. Valuable contact is lost because T.V. programmes are more important to their parents than listening to their children. Some children spend many hours in front of a V.D.U. screen, or wearing headphones when they are out. What kind of memories will they have when they are old – other people's fantasies? What will today's children remember of their school days?

Too many children are being bussed or driven by parents, to very large schools, where they lose their identity and the sense of belonging to a particular community. Added to that is the pressure to achieve certain educational standards, giving the feeling of failure to so many young people; while the general message and impression given by our society is that moral standards don't count. Perhaps it's not surprising that drug dealers come along and pick out, not only the adventurous spirits with too much money, but the dissatisfied, quiet teenagers, who don't get enough attention at home.

I have come to the conclusion that although my school days had its faults, I had a wonderful childhood compared to the children of today.

Chrissie's Thoughts

Is this the school? How far? How far to go?
Rest awhile, boots heavy, can I go slow?
Is this the school? How far, another gate or stile?
Running on, and on, run each tiring mile.

Playground, school, classroom, then allotted seat.
Register, name called out, now all complete.
Prayers, hymns, lessons, playtime, a crowded place.
Out now with brothers, homework, open space.

Smiddy clamour, sparks, hot shoes, hammer blows,
skilfully shapes, scars, fire and metal glows.
Talking smith, cool soak, sizzle, hiss and spits.
Nails on giant shire's shoe. "There lass, now shoe fits."

The workhorse walks easier, as we glance back,
as racing on to moorland, o'er muddy track,
Rough, moor path, farm dogs barking, geese complain,
More farms, gates, fields, heather, mud; one last lane.

Seasons change, winter snow and horse drawn sleigh.
Christmas, concert, party, skating, storm on way.
Spring, Nest building, snowdrops, primroses bloom.
New lambs, boxing hares, wild colts threaten doom.

Frogs breeding, racing. Hawks swoop and larks hover.
Foxes, snakes, badgers, red deer. Eagle, take cover.
Weekend hunting hares and rabbits to stew.
Ploughing's done, fledglings fly, Summer is due.

Heather, wildlife, country smells, colours and sights.
Sounds, lapwing's song, friendship; life delights.
Energy, happiness, family home.
Real in my memory, I'm never alone.

Ruby

The Story I had to Tell

by Ruby

his book was complete, now that I had written a poem about Chrissie that she approved of. Well, I thought it was complete; then we went on a nostalgic run round Deeside and Finzean. This is my own description of that day, so I will be relating these events in my own words and referring to Chrissie as Mum.

The need to have a suitable jacket for the book gave us the excuse for the drive. As my husband was on a Sunday golf outing to Braemar, my brother John came to pick me up at my home in Ellon. Mum was already in the car and I brought my camera in the hope of taking a suitable picture. John decided to take a longer, more interesting route than we would normally have taken and Mum added interesting snippets of old memories as we travelled. This was really meant only for our own ears, as

Mum is very selective about the memories she allows to be printed. As we passed the tourist's driveway to "Haddo House" she commented that she knew that road well.

"In the late twenties your grandfather, and two of your uncles helped to widen and improve the road. During the summer, your grandfather usually managed to get two or three months casual work, either road building or forestry work. After 'The First World War' my mother wouldn't allow Father to go far without her, so the whole family came." There were a few more items of interest, not for inclusion in this book, then we came to Old Meldrum, where my mother was born.

We stopped at the car park in front of the library, while Mum pointed in the direction of a stripped pine shop. She can still see vague outlines and colours, which helps her to recognise familiar places. "It's the shop on that corner. I was born in the flat above, it was tiny but it went with the shop."

I looked at the old shop. "Didn't the baker want the flat for his family, Mum."

"It wasn't a baker's shop, until after we left Old Meldrum. I told you, the flat went with the shop. I have an idea that it was an ironmongers then, but I'm not sure. It must have been doing well, or Father wouldn't have agreed to buy it. Although he wanted us to own our home, he rented the shop and flat at first."

"I didn't know Granda ran a shop here, Mum!"

"We didn't have it for long. Father agreed a price and shook hands on the deal. That was the way things were done in those days. Then a man who wanted the shop offered £25 more. The owner didn't give my father the chance to match the new offer.

The seller didn't even tell Father himself. He may even have been told by the lawyer, when he went to pay for the building. There was very little warning, in no time we had to leave."

"So Grannie and Granda lost their home and their livelihood in one stroke." Mum nodded, then she went on to say that "Later on Father was able to buy a house in Deeside. It was difficult finding a house to buy then, as practically all the land in the countryside was owned by the big estates. I was too young to remember the flat or the shop, as I was only a baby when we left."

We travelled on to Torphins and Mum added a few more old memories along the way. Our main intention was to visit my father's grave at Torphins. I brought flowers and checked whether the rose bush that my husband John planted last Autumn was growing. While we were there I also wanted to visit "The Painters' Bazaar", in the "Learney Hall." I still hoped to buy a ready made picture for the book cover. There was nothing really suitable, so we headed for "Finzean School".

My original idea was to use an old photograph of the school for the cover, but I have been unable to locate a suitable one. The school is now a modern building, built about thirty years ago, on the old school garden which my uncles helped cultivate. Growing vegetables was taken seriously by the old schools. We walked through the old playground and my mother showed us where Bigfoot tripped her up. She also described how the biplane flew towards the school, startling all the pupils. The building there has modern styled windows, so it's not much like the original building. Further on Mum pointed out the smiddy and the three and a half mile short cut home. We stopped for tea and sandwiches opposite the "Finzean Post Office Shop", which was open. I decided to enquire there about old photographs of the area.

I introduced myself to Jill McGregor, the owner, who suggested a local man who might be able to help. I was delighted to receive our first firm order for copies of this book. This was a very memorable and exciting moment for me. At times I worry that I will let Mum down, so Jill's kindness probably meant more to me than she realised. Back in the car Mum decided that we wouldn't visit Robin Callander, for information on old photographs.

"I'm not bothering people, complete strangers, on a Sunday, to ask for favours. Anyway, I think your brother should paint a picture for the book cover. He's a good enough artist." What a good idea! If he does that, and gets it painted in time, who am I to argue? I asked John to take us to the old house next.

I wanted to take a photograph of my grandparents house, for my own album, while it is still there. This brought me an interesting and unexpected result; and the whole point of this story. While we took photographs of the old house, Mum sat in the car remembering events triggered by the visit. One of these events, which she particularly wanted me to record, but not to have published, was preceded by an order of, you must not publish this story. Promise me you will not publish this story.

"Why not." I don't usually argue but I had a feeling that this story was special.

"Because I was only two and a half years old, or maybe I

was three and a half. This book is about my school days, not before then."

"If it's that good, I'm sure we could make an exception."

"No. Anyway, I was with your aunt and she doesn't want to be included in the book." Even if you don't use her name, the story would be embarrassing for me. So promise me you won't write this story." Reluctantly I agreed.

"We spent the summer near Braemar one year. Although it's not far from here it wasn't practical for Father to travel to work from here. He worked for the sawmill, felling trees. I remember walking along one of these narrow, country roads with an older sister. I can't remember why we were there, but I remember a large old car which was parked, partly off the road. We were walking past the car on the other side of the road, which meant we were still quite close to the car. We didn't stare at the car, but it was obvious to my sister that they were part of a hunting party, having a picnic. It was probably after August, 12th, about 1922 or 1923. Now, I don't want this story published, however interesting you find it!"

"O.K. Mum." John was muttering something like, "Oh, just get on with the story."

"We walked almost past the car when an old man with a beard called us over. He was a pleasant old man with a kindly manner. I took an immediate liking to him, which was unusual for me. He asked if we lived in the area. My sister explained why we were there. The old man looked at me and remarked that I was a beautiful child. Particularly my hair, and 'What an unusual colour of hair'. We continued on our way, but were called back by the old man. 'I have something for you!' He called. We didn't want to take anything from strangers and stood still where we were, uncertain about what to do. Then a chauffeur came over with apples, saying that they were left over from the picnic. My sister said, 'Please thank the kind gentleman for the apples.'

"The chauffeur looked amused. 'Do you know who the kind gentleman is?'

"'No,' replied my big sister, looking rather uneasy.

"'That kind gentleman is your king. King George the Fifth. I'll pass on your message.'

"The King smiled at us again, and waved. Then we walked off down the road.

"Now do you see why I don't want this story to be told."

"No I don't, but if you don't want the story told then I won't include it in the book." We set off home after this story and I fully intended keeping my word, but I can't. A herd of wild colts won't keep me from telling anyone who is prepared to listen, that "My mother's hair was once admired by the ruling monarch." Sorry Mum.

Appreciations and Apologies

I would like to thank everyone who has given me encouragement and practical help in producing this book. In particular special thanks to Librarian John Smith and former writer in residence at Aberdeen Central Library, Todd McEwen. Lenders of photographs also deserve my appreciation.

Angus Farquharson of Finzean was particularly encouraging in a letter he sent in reply to a preview of the stories relating to Joseph Farquharson of Finzean. Angus described the stories as "A Delightful account of a bygone age". He also informed me that although Joseph was Laird of Finzean, "He and Violet would not claim to be Lord and Lady Farquharson, but merely Joseph and Violet Farquharson of Finzean". After giving this information careful thought, I decided to leave the incorrect title as it was previously given. These memories are intended to be a description of the events and of the time, as I saw them. Local people referred to "The laird and his lady, or Lord and Lady Farquharson" at the time. I don't think anyone would object to me remembering them in this way.

I sincerely apologise for any mistakes I have made while telling these stories. They are all a true account of my own experiences. However, they are events as seen through the eyes of a child, a very long time ago and nobody is perfect. I have avoided giving names where these stories could upset or embarrass anyone. Although most people in my book have passed on, their descendants could still be embarrassed by past events.

Lastly, I would like to thank you, the reader, for giving meaning to an old woman's last few years. I hope you enjoy sharing my memories.

Chrissie Gibson